THE TIMELESS LAND

THE TIMELESS LAND

The creative spirit in Cornwall

DENYS VAL BAKER

ADAMS & DART

SBN 239. 00132. x
First published in 1973
by Adams & Dart, 1a Queen Square, Bath, Somerset
Text printed by Redwood Press Ltd, Trowbridge, Wiltshire
Illustrations printed at The Pitman Press, Bath
Bound in Great Britain

Contents

List of Illustrations

The illustrations in this book are taken from various past issues of the CORNISH REVIEW, and reproduced by kind permission of the publishers of that magazine.

The drawing on the dust-jacket is by Margo Maeckleberghe

FOR MY SON MARTIN
with love

Preface

EVER SINCE, a quarter of a century ago, I first came to live in Cornwall I have been fascinated by two things—by Cornwall itself, 'the timeless land', and by the tremendous amount of creative work going on within its boundaries. Living in various parts of the county—in a castle at Portquin, a converted cowshed on the side of Trencrom Hill, a haunted cottage on the Land's End cliffs, an old vicarage at St Hilary, a beach house at St Ives, and now a creekside mill on the River Fowey—I have come to realise the strange and often subterranean link between Cornwall and its creativity. As a Welshman, and therefore a fellow Celt, and as a writer myself I have, of course, been particularly 'sensitised' to the whole subject: but I really do not think you need to be either a Celt or an artist to be aware of the strange and compelling powers embedded in Cornwall's granite body. Ask almost any holidaymaker just why he has come to Cornwall—more important, as is so often the case, why he comes back again and again—and you will get the same sort of vague and indefinite answer which is all, I fear, even I am able to provide in this book. But because it is vague, do not dismiss it: in a timeless land which still belongs remarkably to the shadows of the past, of other worlds, the only possible answers must be intangible. If Cornwall could be explained, it would cease to be Cornwall.

When in 1949 I first founded the CORNISH REVIEW I did so precisely because of my growing awareness of the strange qualities of Cornwall which resulted in so many creative artists being drawn down to England's western heel. During almost a quarter of a century since then the CORNISH REVIEW has been able to publish and reproduce art and literature of remarkable variety and standard—far beyond the normal level to be found in an ordinary English 'county'. For this book I have drawn heavily upon extracts and quotations from some of our magazine's contents, because indeed I could hardly wish for better evidence to prove my case! But I have also endeavoured to take the reader into the past as well, showing how many great artists of various kinds have been just as influenced by Cornwall in other centuries. The names, indeed, sound rather like a roll call of fame: Tennyson, Dickens, Hardy, Turner, Du Maurier, Spring, Betjeman, Hepworth, Nicholson, Wallis, Berlin, Lanyon etc. But I have also quoted from many less illustrious creative workers because fame has really very little to do with the matter. What concerns me and has done now for 25 years and will no doubt continue to do so is the whole mysterious aspect of it all. *Why* does Cornwall effect people so profoundly, often indeed dramatically? What alchemy is present that so stirs the creative spirit?

Needless to say I am only too well aware that in attempting to answer these questions in this short book I have, at best, only partially succeeded. But at least I may have achieved two things. I will have fulfilled my own long-standing ambition to 'have a go' at a difficult but fascinating subject—and perhaps I may help to introduce a few more people to the truly mysterious and magical world of 'the timeless land.'

Denys Val Baker
St. Buryan, 1972

I

The Mystery and the Magic

IN ORDER to understand the influence of the county upon creative workers of all kinds it might be as well first to identify just what we mean by the term, Cornwall. From almost any point of view it quickly becomes apparent that although officially included in the country known as England, Cornwall can hardly be said to be part of that country. Down all the centuries—from those far-off times when it was part of the south-west peninsula of Dumnonia right up to the present, when its local authorities have just successfully managed to preserve its separate identity in the face of all the immense regional reshuffles —Cornwall has been notably different, a place of its own. It would be difficult to drum up much romantic excitement about 'going to Essex' or 'going to Bucks' or 'going to Leicestershire'—yet even to this day there remains an intangible yet very real romanticism about 'going to Cornwall'. It is going west, towards the sun, into the mysterious land of Lyonesse, into another world. It is a difference even applying to personalities: as W. Gore Allen, editor of the DEVON JOURNAL once commented:

> 'Whenever I cross the Tamar, journeying East or West, I am surprised afresh that one of the world's least penetrable frontiers should be made evident by so small a width of water. Cornwall and Devon could send plenipotentaries almost to clasp hands across the stream: yet if these men were truly representative of their two counties they would turn away, the Cornishmen choleric, the Devon men resigned, to admit their mutual and complete incomprehension. The differences are mental, spiritual and emotional.'

It is not really surprising that there should be such a sharp difference between the Cornish and their nearest neighbours, for the simple fact is that with their Celtic background the Cornish have far less in common with the entire English nation than they have, for example with their cousins in Wales, Scotland and Ireland. What is even more interesting is that the similarity goes beyond character and human personality and extends even into geology. If you want to find cliffs like the Cornish cliffs, moorland like the Cornish moorland, lonely and bleak hills like the Cornish hills, then you will find them not in Bucks. or Berks., Kent or Herts., Worcestershire or Lancashire—but in the Western Isles of Scotland, among the mountains of Snowdonia, on the Atlantic-washed coast of Southern Ireland. And of course, just as those regions are famous for their romantic historical associations, so is Cornwall impregnated with its great legends—King Arthur and his Knights, Tristan and Iseult, and so forth. Perhaps, too, it is not irrelevant that it was from Cornwall there sprang the last rebellion on English soil, the Western Rising of 1549.

Cornwall, in short, in the face of all the mass centralisation of our modern society, has remained stubbornly *different*. There are some people who believe that if only the Cornish language had been preserved for everyday use then the county might have attained the same relative independence as Wales or Scotland (and indeed in a forlorn attempt to recapture such a situation, immense efforts are now being made to spread a knowledge of the old Cornish language). But surely this is rather to miss the whole point. Cornwall does not need to create differences to emphasise its apartness from the rest of England. It *is* apart, solidly and unmistakably, and in the fullest geographical sense. Even its position of being the most westerly of all English counties at once puts it, literally, 'out on a limb'. Then again, no other English county has such a long coastline—in no other English county are even the inland areas so close to the sea. Sea-washed and impregnated in this unusual way, then of course Cornwall at once becomes apart, different from the rest of England. After all, we have only to remember the fabulous legend of Lyonesse—that vast area of forest land between Cornwall and the Isles of Scilly which was, as John Norden wrote in his *Speculi Britanniae Pars* in 1584, 'swallowed vp by the deuowring sea'. This is no mere fantasy; there *are* many records of submarine forests, at Mount's Bay, at Mevagissey. A diarist noted in 1777, 'Off from Seaton, a valley between Ramehead and Looe, there is to be seen on a clear day in the bottom of the sea, a league from the shore, a whole wood of timber on its side, uncorrupted'. A submarine forest *does* lie off Looe in Milandreath Bay; when heavy seas strip away the sand tree trunks are visible, reddish and decayed.

Here we come close to the true identification of Cornwall. It combines forcefully and self-evidently an extraordinary blend of romance and reality, myth and matter, fantasy and fact. The reasons that most people are so affected by Cornwall—even to the extent, like Walter de La Mare, of being literally frightened when they cross the River Tamar into this unknown territory—is that they have in front of their very eyes all the physical evidence for the mystery and magic that so enthrals and troubles them. It is one thing to read as romantic fiction old stories about the Cornish giants of Trencrom and St Michael's Mount who used to toss rocks to one another with the same ease that a child might toss a pebble; but climb up to the top of Trencrom Hill, look around at the ground positively studded with great boulders lying just as they might have done if thrown from a distance, and you might begin to wonder. An interesting comment on this subject was once made by the folklore historian, A.F.C. Hillstead:

> Let us consider for a moment some of the tales of the Cornish giants. To the foreigner they are no more than impossible inventions of primitive minds; just fairy tales for nought else than simple entertainment. To the student, however, these numerous legends seem as if they offer romance tempered with reality. There are too many stories of Cornish giants not to have a significance greater than that of mere fiction. Indeed we may well ask why so many? I seek no further than symbolism for the answer. Cornwall is a land of extremes. Its people are both fair and dark and one sees many of immense stature. In its sheltered valleys there is a vegetation so luxurious that we are reminded of the semi-tropical regions. On the other hand, winter brings to the bleak uplands winds like whetted knives; the snow flurries sourly and he who of necessity has to visit the well-head may find the chain is caked with ice, the handle clotted in rime and the ewer's dribblings frozen as they touch the cobbled ground. There are sandy bays lapped by the mildest of blue seas, and mighty granite bastions whose feet are forever snarled and fretted by the suck and surge of Atlantic waves. Therefore is it not natural that these opposing features should have been symbolised by giants? Giants who fought each other with the fury of the wind; who spread devastation in the manner of a tidal wave yet were known to have moments when they played like normal boys and girls. These stories, then, are more than idle imaginings. They are descriptive of the land, the sea, and the many vagaries of the weather.

One could give endless examples of the way in which Cornwall provides proof to back its myths. Who, for instance, standing beside the waters of the strange and lonely Dozmary Pool on Bodmin Moor, would have much difficulty in imagining that dramatic event when an arm was raised above the waters of the lake to clutch the jewelled hilt of the magic sword, Excalibur? Some years ago I lived in a small castle on the cliffs of Portquin, on the North Coast of Cornwall, and while there learned that the whole of the local fishing fleet once sunk around the jagged rocky coast, and that often the anguished cries of the drowning men could be heard above the sound of the waves. Was it entirely my imagination that sometimes, as the sun lowered in the sky and a grey seething swell came booming in, I did indeed hear forlorn voices? Who can say? Does it really matter? The cliffs, the rocks, the majestic seas

—against such a background, disasters of traumatic proportions were entirely conceivable. In Cornwall, over which hovers a mist of the distant past, anything can happen.

Geographically, then, Cornwall provides its own evidence to justify the theme of this book. That is to say, while of course much of the mystery and brooding sense of the past must often be perceived by instinct, nevertheless we can see in the very landscape itself, and especially the sea-washed coastline, something of what it is that so stimulates and encourages the creative mind. It has been said, for instance, that the cliffs from Treryn Dinas to Land's End, most of them under National Trust ownership, are the most beautiful in Great Britain. As beautiful as the cliffs themselves are some of the rock formations at their feet, rocks that sometimes seem almost sentient in their attitudes, hence the nick names, 'the Armed Knight', 'the Shark's Fin', 'Dr Syntax'. There is a sense of grim unrelenting battle about this Land's End coastline. Even on a hot, cloudless June day the sea never gives the impression of being quite at peace. The waves lapping around the salt-flecked rocks, splashing the seagulls and cormorants as they sunbathe, have an angry irritable flick to them, the rocks and cliffs themselves carry the same sense of inward seething strength, perhaps anger. They are no part of twentieth-century civilisation; they belong to an immense and imponderable past.

From Mousehole you can walk all the way to Land's End over the cliffs, dropping down into picturesque Lamorna Cove, then up and down again into tiny Penberth and over the cliffs past Logan Rock and down to Porthcurno, home of Cornwall's whitest sands and the cable station to America; on past the Minack Theatre, hewn incredibly out of the granite sides of the cliff; past St Levan Church and through the fishing village of Porthgwarra where the way to the sea leads through a hole in the cliff; round Gwennap Head and the coastguard-hut perched looking far out to the Atlantic and the hooting buoy; along a twisting, rambling coastline, with a sheer drop down to angry looking rocks and stones until, rounding Nanjizel Bay, the walker comes in sight of the Enys Dodman rock and the Longships Lighthouse standing sentinel a mile-and-a-half out to sea.

Northwards, after Sennen Cove with its beautiful white sand beach the coast winds out to the Cape, and past the dreadful Brisons rocks, responsible for the wrecks of so many unfortunate ships which have run in too close to land; on past Kenidjack with its ruined castle; past a number of narrow valleys and coves which once led to prosperous tin and copper mines, Bottallack, Wheal Bal, Levant (where a collapse of the shaft running out under the sea-bed brought death to hundreds of Cornish miners.) All the way along this rugged and lonely coastline a common sight is the gaunt skeleton frame of defunct mine-heads, long ago stripped of their wood for fuel.

Further along towards the St Ives end of the peninsula is Gurnard's Head, which offers some of the finest rock climbing in Britain and is regularly used by various climbing clubs. Honeysuckle sometimes grows on the cliffs at Gurnard's Head in the spring, though as like as not they will be whisked away by the wind. From Gurnard's Head past Zennor towards Clodgy Point and the sudden sandy stretches of St Ives, the coastline is as beautiful as on the southern side, but somehow more remote and brooding. It is here that one is haunted by an indescribable feeling of solitude. Drive along the road that climbs out of St Ives and turns westwards towards Zennor and you will understand what I mean. The meeting of the two smooth expanses of land and sea creates an even larger and more disturbing vastness, in which a tree on the land is as rare a sight as a ship on the sea.

So much for a fragmentary stretch of Cornish coastline. The descriptions could be extended all the way up the striking North Coast, with its incredible variety of stupendous cliffs interspaced by vast stretches of sands like Gwithian, where a whole church was found buried under the sands—and not even the most poetic or purple passages could necessarily do justice to many parts of the opposite South coast, especially such desolate and fearsome areas as the Lizard, with the nearby Manacles on which have died so many fine ships. A poet's eye, too, would be needed to do justice to such settings as St Austell Bay—Mevagissey to one side, Fowey to the other, and in the background the man-made yet haunting images of the china-clay tips, rising like white mountains.

But Cornwall is not merely coastline: it has an interior, too, even though hardly any part is more than a few miles from the sea. In its own way that interior is just as remarkable as all those hundreds of miles of wandering beaches and coves and harbours and cliffs—as anyone would agree who has, for example, wandered among the ancient tin-mine no-man's-lands of St Day and Redruth. Then there are those St Austell claypits to which I have already referred, and whose imagery features so strikingly in the poems of Cornwall's leading poet Jack Clemo:

> My Destiny is drawn
>   Sharp as the prongs
> Of a clay-tip against the dawn,
>   Unsoftened by the lark's song.

Two gleaming fingers on the white snout,
   Grotesque above the clotted cone
Of carnal doubt;
   They are Dogma's radiant bone.

Bodmin Moor is another notable symbol of the weirdness, the out-of-the-ordinariness, of the Cornish interior. Here is the Cornish Everest, Brown Willy, 1,375 ft high—and neighbouring Rough Tor, only 63 ft lower. From their pinnacles you can on a clear day glimpse the Bristol Channel on one side and the English Channel on the other. It was from this position, 'the roof of Cornwall', that Cornish art critic Michael Tresillian once reflected upon how the imagination stirred, and the dividing line between fact and fiction became blurred:

I have sat in a horse's saddle on Brown Willy grateful for a sturdy, sure-footed cob, and watched the different worlds of Devon and Cornwall fade into a morning haze; a day when the wind slept and only birds and animals moved. I have wedged myself between rocks on Rough Tor and attempted to hide from the invisible knife of the wind—and both times I have been conscious of the same fact. Cornwall is a draughtsman's country. There is a sense of geometry in the landscape and even the sun, filtering through, intensifying the colours, cannot alter it.

Above all, the interior of Cornwall has a hard, implacable base. Dig a hole anywhere and you will eventually strike granite. Granite forms the spine of Cornwall—granite *is* Cornwall, in so many ways. And this, too, is part of the strangeness of the county—part of the difference. It is a world of stark rock-like shapes looming out of bogs and moors, of weird cloud-formations racing across storm-bound skies—a world of shadow and substance, marvel and miracle. On Bodmin Moor, on Carn Brea at Redruth, on Trencrom Hill and a dozen other pinnacles (where on Midsummer Night Eves, appropriately enough, bonfires are lit), it is literally impossible to feel one is in any ordinary, normal sort of background. And the same, too, of course, goes for the sea-washed cliffs of Bedruthan Steps, of Hell's Mouth near Hayle, of Lamorna or Treen or Porthgwarra—of the Lizard, Kynance Cove, Mullion—of almost anywhere along the long coastline.

Small wonder then, that against such a background the Cornish people themselves should develop essentially as an isolated race, their past at their elbow continuously. The Victorian novelist, George Meredith, put it rather well:

The past of their lives has lost neither face nor voice behind the shroud, nor are the passions of the flesh, nor is the animate soul wanting to it. Other races forfeit infancy, forfeit youth and manhood, with their progression to the wisdom age may bestow. These have each stage always alive, quick at a word, a scent, a sound to conjure up scenes, in spirit and in flame.

The Cornish people themselves are like their land, an old and knowing race, withdrawn to strangers, living as much in the past as the present; without, in fact, much creative inspiration of their own yet with a quick response to things of that nature—what has been called 'a reaction to a sensitised soil.' Rosalie Glyn Grylls, who coined that phrase, once summed up her native character very entertainingly in an article she wrote for the CORNISH REVIEW:

The thing about the Cornish is that they are not nice; exciting and attractive but not nice. They have colour enough to turn the spectacles of most onlookers pink but it is not fast to light. The impulsiveness that goes as far as magnanimity does not sustain generosity; the devotion, loyal for fanaticism, has no fidelity; the forthcomingness keeps much more back than reticence—like an ice-berg two thirds under the water, if there were not anything less like an ice-berg than any Celt . . . Where does it go, then, all the colour? The warm tones of manner, the light and shade of speech?. The colour goes into the personality. Almost one might say it is enough for the Cornish to be Cornish; but not quite for they have a full measure of Celtic discontent. The energy that makes for colourfulness goes into the business of living—always a hard one in Cornwall—the fervour into congregational worship, into a personal relationship with omnipotence, not into embellishing its dwelling-place; the enterprise into seeking fortunes afield.

This is not, however, a book about the Cornish people. It is not they who have created the timeless land that has exerted such a strange and strong influence on so many artists. It is, in fact, the timeless land that has created the Cornish people—as yet one more manifestation of its strange and brooding and very real influence. To that extent it is worth noting that this is the kind of human background of Cornwall, these are the kind of people with whom, over the years, so many 'foreigners', and especially artists, have intermingled. It is all part of the general and unending mystery of Cornwall.

II

The Creative County

AS I SAID earlier, when Walter de la Mare first visited Cornwall his immediate reaction was one of unease: in fact, in his own words he did not feel safe until he had crossed the river Tamar back into Devon. Another poet, John Heath-Stubbs, after living on the edge of the wild North Cornish cliffs at Gurnard's Head, wrote passionately;

This a hideous and wicked country
Sloping to hateful sunsets and the end of time . . .

And yet another writer, the novelist Ruth Manning-Sanders, has recalled vividly long walks out on the Land's End cliffs in the twilight of a wintry afternoon when nothing was to be seen but the huge dim shapes of the silently withdrawing cliffs and the rhythmically winking eye of the Longships Lighthouse:

> It is then that the drowned sailors of the past can be heard hailing their names above the moaning of the waters. It is then that the sense of the primordial, the strange and the savage, the unknown, the very long ago, fills the dusk with something that is akin to dread. It is then that the place becomes haunted: a giant heaves grey limbs from his granite bed, a witch sits in that stone chair on the cliff . . .

Here, in a few phrases, is established a vivid image of Cornwall, or the Kingdom of Kernow as it was once known. It is a place apart, a world of its own, full indeed of a spirit and atmosphere of 'the very long ago'. Once, when climbing to the top of a hill above St Ives, a man said to a little boy, 'This was where the Druids worshipped their idol gods'. When the boy asked, 'How long ago.' the man answered vaguely, 'about 100 years, I suppose.' Past and present, moments and centuries, all are entangled and interwoven in Cornwall. Eternity is contained in 100 years. And this is reflected even in the people, of whom George Meredith once observed that the past is at their elbow continuously: 'the past of their lives has lost neither face nor voice behind the shroud, nor are the passions of the flesh, nor is the animate soul, wanting it.' But above all it is the physical landscape that makes the first striking, indeed overwhelming, impact. Suddenly one is surrounded by a romantic, wild, majestic awe inspiring, mysterious and in some ways private universe, whose forlorn granite monuments are still to be spied in the form of quoits and tombs, cairns and standing stones, crosses and cromlechs. It is by no means necessary to watch the sunset at Land's End to become aware of this strange feeling of a brooding past. If you stand on the promontory of Cape Cornwall, or on the remains of the cliff castle at Treen Dinas—if you wander among the crumbled remains of ancient settlements at Chysauster or Porthmeor in the Zennor area—if you visit such strange remnants of the neolithic and bronze ages as Lanyon Quit near Madron or the Men-an-tol monument in a croft nearby—indeed, if you explore almost any of the remoter areas of West Cornwall you will, unless completely devoid of imagination, experience an emotional response, a sense of the supernatural, that you will not easily forget. Upon your reaction to this impact may well depend your whole future; there are innumerable cases of people (of all classes and creeds) who have come to Cornwall for a holiday—and stayed a lifetime. That is the sort of dramatic, indeed melodramatic influence that may be exerted by England's most westerly corner.

Perhaps, then, it is hardly surprising that creative artists of all kinds have been drawn, almost as if by some powerful magnet, to Cornwall. Creation itself is a most mysterious process: what more natural than like should attract like, that men and women engaged in the creative act should be drawn to an area where, as a seer once put it, the veil is very thin? In a land drenched in legends, inpregnated with memories of barbaric and druidic rituals—whose shores look out even now over that famous lost land of Lyonesse—how could there fail to be an underlying current of occult power? After all, scientists have confirmed the high radio-activity of Cornwall's granite—surely we may accept artists' evidence of an even more mysterious and secret power? It is, then, only natural that creative artists, with their more highly developed imaginations and intuitive powers, should react most immediately. Yet, as I have said, people from all walks of life have a similar reaction. Sir George P. Christopher, chairman of the Hain Steamship Company of Hayle, once described stopping his car on a Cornish moor and feasting his eyes on those great rough bits of granite in a spirit of reverence for the message they conveyed from their rugged grandeur:

> Let anyone stand in Zennor Churchtown and look up at the rocky hills lying behind the road to St. Ives and his heart is hard as the granite itself if he is not moved to see something more than a mere profusion of the wastage of nature; and in doing so, to breathe a benediction upon it all for the sense of strength it seems to be giving—indeed always to have given. Or let him stand on the top of

Trencrom and look down on all sides upon the quiet land beneath him and between him and the distant sea; on the great stones all around him; at the sheltering rock bastions of Tregonning, Godolphin, Carn Brea, Trink and Trendrine. Or, stand on Gwithian Head looking inland to Trencrom itself, which, with the lesser Worvas Hill, stands sentinel over the clustering habitations of Lelant, Carbis Bay and St. Ives. All these breathe into a Cornishman something of their own calm, their timelessness and the solid front with which they have faced the ages since they were formed.

What Sir George Christopher sought to express has been captured, often much more vividly, by a wide variety of artists. The wheel has certainly turned full circle from the time when judges refused to hold their assizes farther into Cornwall than Launceston, on the Cornish-Devon border, because they were literally afraid to penetrate beyond the sinister mysteries of Bodmin Moor In the past century Cornwall has been explored in all its facets, by pen and brush, stone and clay, weave and wood—reflected and captured in a hundred guises. Moreover, there is a formidable array of witnesses—from the great landscape painter, Turner, to our most famous Poet Laureate, Alfred Lord Tennyson; from Charles Dickens, who accompanied his fellow novelist Wilkie Collins on a tramp around the Cornish coast, to later best-selling novelists such as Daphne Du Maurier and Howard Spring, Walter Greenwood and Winston Graham, Hammond Innes and Margaret Kennedy; from internationally known painters such as Ben Nicholson and Christopher Wood to local primitives such as Alfred Wallis and Mary Jewells; from sculptors like Sven Berlin and Barbara Hepworth to wood carvers like Dennis Mitchell and Robin Nance; and including craftsmen of great skill and renown such as Bernard Leach, the potter, Francis Cargeeg, the copper worker, Archibald Carne, worker in wrought iron, and many others. Such artists have testified, both in their work and in their words, to the strange but dynamic influence which their physical surroundings, i.e. Cornwall, have had upon their acts of creation.

This was once put very well by Sven Berlin when he suggested that in Cornwall the terraced landscape of the little fishing towns and the geological nature of the rock at once became operative, along with the submarine cargo of shells, skulls, fish and plants, in orientating one's vision back to the fundamental shapes of nature. . . . This, added to the peculiar influence Cornwall had upon the unconscious mind of man, brought into line once more the ancient forces of creation that have a close affinity with the spirit of life. In such an environment the artist found it became possible for modern man to make a statement about humanity—penetrating its mechanical armour and seeing it once again as a dynamic part of the universal order governed by the mystery of God. Sven Berlin went on to try and put his experiences into words:

When the sea gets into a leg I am carving what excitement there is! It goes charging through the whole of the stone, and a man, as if by magic, is transformed into an ocean with rocks and tides, shells and caves—a sea-dragon. The whole galaxy of one's experience pours in upon him: one works in a kind of dream as though someone else is making the image. Is it not true that the doors of life, when open, release shapes and forces hidden inside us for ages? Be that as it may, there is no *reasonable* explanation of what happens . . . All I know is that it was Cornwall that helped to release and develop my ability to create something living out of stone. After a while I became so deeply rooted in the Cornish landscape that to go and carve in a city, in a forest, or among mountains would so alter my vision that it would probably be impossible to work for a considerable time.

Yet another aspect of the living nature of Cornish landscape was traced, in both his work and words, by the late Peter Lanyon, the Cornish painter, who spoke of a main force in Cornwall that was centrifugal and centripetal, a giving out and a taking in. In extremes this meant a complete trust and desire to give absolutely everything and a converse withdrawal, a returning to a protective native envelope. From this attitude of seeing Cornwall both from inside, as a Cornishman, and outside, as a painter, Peter Lanyon attempted to describe the true nature of the landscape:

From Wicca to Levant the coastline emerges out of carns and bracken and cultivated greenland, revealing on its varied faces a sea history and a land history of men within and without and a commerce of man with the weather. Here in a small stretch of headland, cove and Atlantic adventure, the most distant histories are near the surface as if the final convulsion of rock upheaval and cold incision, setting in a violent sandwich of strata, had directed the hide and seek of Celtic pattern.

Cornwall's creative influence is by no means confined to the wandering coastline, majestic and awe-inspiring though that may be. Another painter, Lionel Miskin, has found his inspiration elsewhere. Indeed he deliberately turned his back on the sea.

In summer it's possible to walk round the harbour and see it murdered, travestied, souped up and watered down on twenty or more canvases, jelloid boats jostling in watered Quink against cardboard quays . . . no love could survive such a prostitution.

Bodmin Moor, on the other hand, shares with the china clay country a certain starkness, an almost brutally present structure suggesting petrified waves, crested at the tors, otherwise in deep wide undulations. The deep recessions of ochre and golden grass in the winter and of greens in spring only lightly cover a sculpture you know to be black as iron or bronze, for planted or cut for peat this blackness is laid bare in a geometric patch-work that is as dark as that of the clay country a few miles further west is white. Even the cattle on the Moor tend to be black.

I've painted both on the high land of the Moor and in the valley running down to Golitha Falls and I've experienced a selfish pleasure . . . the place doesn't seem to interest many other painters. An advantage hitherto unknown to landscape painters is the ability to paint from a car in really wild weather, to look out at the extraordinary shapes of clouds building up on the Moor for a powerful storm, to see the shapes of rocks or hill appear and disappear in clouds and watch the ignitions of the sun on their surfaces. Clouds are as fine as any subjects known to figurative art, a visibly transforming sculpture, and the light of wild wet weather in Cornwall far excels that of acceptably fine sunshine and cluster-blue skies.

As another painter, Charles Simpson, once commented, 'There is an atmosphere of Age in Cornwall and the early history of man seems to brood over these hills and moors where ponies wander freely, foxes bark, animals call and only man wants to hide . . .'

And yet another painter, this time a Cornishman, Dick Gilbert, put it like this:

Cornwall works on me. Take this one valley here. If I stayed here a hundred years I shouldn't have exhausted its painting possibilities. Maybe it's just because I'm a Cornishman, but you get this feeling of place. When you go away and come back you get a strong sort of realisation that you're home. The train comes across the bridge over the Tamar, you've been sleeping in the compartment, and you suddenly wake up—'I'm home!'

The Cornish landscape exhibits a constantly changing occurrence, it has a large visual depth or distance, in other counties the land is frequently at a distance, but the visual depth is small . . . the sort of space one gets between the thumb and the index finger, when held at arm's length. To get it another way, one sees little land and a lot of sky. The sky usually predominates one's visual experience of landscape, but in Cornwall there's more land in the visual experience. Cornwall's ideal for me.

This almost physical influence of Cornwall upon the art of creation was once commented on, in a different artistic sphere, by the playwright Nora Ratcliffe when she was invited to write a play especially for performance at the famous Minack Theatre, built on the cliffs near Land's End. She found that the theatre literally haunted her: it demanded its own play, and yet she recognised that whatever play was put on, the Atlantic Ocean would be the main actor. In the end Miss Ratcliffe wrote a version of *Tristan and Iseult*:

The play couldn't have been written anywhere else but at the Minack; not only so that one could check the staging, but so that the sea, the gulls, the changing light could find their way into the imagery of the play itself: tilted wing of a gull, black as the rock's shadow, torn through the rock's teeth . . .

'The play couldn't have been written anywhere else . . .' Just as the picture could not have been painted anywhere else; nor the stone made living, the words made meaningful, the poem brought to perfection. Behind everything, over everything, inside everything, we discern the mysterious influence of Cornwall. Even the craft-workers, often more prosaic in their work, have testified to that same influence, as in an account by an embroideress, Erma Harvey James, of her childhood spent at Hayle, in West Cornwall; of how from that time onwards the memory of shells and seaweed and fierce frail wings seen against sand and sun-pierced water formed an unconscious bias towards a particular emphasis, a personal conception of reality, which was to emerge years later with the recognition of the remote connection between these images and the texture of thread on linen. 'The past then was a source of richness, like buried treasure, which having lain in silence and darkness now became accessible.'

It must indeed be a strange land that has laid its mysterious touch upon so many people, such a variety of artists. *What* has made Cornwall such a strange world? *Why* has it drawn so many creative artists? In *which* manner has it inspired and influenced their work? *How* have they reflected that influence in their finished creations? Is the veil indeed worn so thin in the Kingdom of Kernow that by living and working there creative artists are nearer to occult powers that (perhaps even without their knowledge) provide some extra stimulation? Just what does it all mean and reflect, this strange, perhaps unique interweaving of artist and atmosphere, of landscape and work, of sea and granite, image and epithet?

These are all, ultimately, questions without answer. And perhaps it is precisely for this reason, because there remains in Cornwall, room for man's eternal quest for the unknown, that so many artists have been, are, and I feel sure always will be drawn there.

III

Painters' Paradise

PAINTING is so popular in Cornwall as to be almost an industry in itself. With the possible exception of London there is nowhere else in Britain where there are so many professional artists living and working. St Ives, Newlyn, Mousehole, Lamorna Cove, Sennen Cove, the Lizard, Falmouth, Fowey, Mevagissey, Polperro, Looe, Tintagel, Boscastle, Port Isaac, Padstow, Newquay, Truro—in almost every corner of the county, working in converted fish-cellars, in wide-windowed lofts, in old-fashioned wooden studios and in bright new concrete ones built to specification, artists of many outlooks and techniques have not only made homes but in many cases reputations. The list of famous names, past and present, is indeed an impressive one: Turner, Whistler, Sickert, John, Munnings, Nicholson, Park, Lanyon, Hepworth. . . . Inevitably one asks the question: Why?

The explanation is a mixture of material and mystical, factual and fantastical, all equally important. The climate, the brilliant light, the almost Mediterranean blue of the sea, the fascinating formations of rocks and cliffs, hills and valleys, sand and pebble stones—these are some of the more obvious attractions. So, too, the comparative freedom and easiness of life in a small but surprisingly cosmopolitan town such as St Ives or Polperro, as compared to most English provincial towns: the congenial atmosphere of working and living among large groups of fellow artists; the facilities of numerous art galleries and showrooms, dozens of art societies and clubs; and last but by no means least a sympathetic local population and Press, conditioned by several decades of growing up alongside art colonies, so that what might seem an oddity in some other part of Britain has come to be taken for granted in Cornwall.

Yes, *but* . . . Surely there is something else? Something less easily explained and put into words, yet with perhaps just as strong an influence on artists as the magnetic pull, granite often exerts on ship's compasses? There is, indeed, and how better to attempt to capture this unknown quantity than by asking the artists themselves? Jack Pender, a native of Mousehole and a leading member of the Penwith and Newlyn Society of Artists quoted in the CORNISH REVIEW:

Oh yes, there's a spiritual something here. I have met different people who have reacted to it in different ways: those who came for a week and stayed years, and those who couldn't stand it and cleared out quickly. Through the war, art training and later teaching, I was out of Cornwall for twenty years . . . this thing gradually grew on me, I experienced it when I came home on leave or holiday . . . it became an obsession. I *had* to get back. Even when out of Cornwall I found myself painting pictures of Cornwall, subjects I had remembered. The whole thing became very intense.

For me the Cornish landscape means a lot. I've been to other places where it's been lush and soft but I haven't felt altogether happy in it. The openness of the landscape appeals to me, this sense of being on the top, exposed, and yet, in a way, it makes you vulnerable, but in the present state of international art, environment and place seem to have less importance.

My roots are deep under the granite walls and quays. Maybe I'm too comfortable, maybe I should have shaken them loose. This is *my* area, but it may have had a bad effect. Perhaps I should have gone to some exotic place, somewhere with very different colours and subjects . . . I'd probably be frightened stiff. I like it in Cornwall. In Mousehole I know everybody and they know everything about me. I find myself tapping a wall and saying to myself: 'You're an old friend. How many times have I tapped you since I was a boy?'

Another Cornish-born painter, Margo Maeckleberghe of Penzance, when asked in the same interview, 'Why does Cornwall attract painters?'

I've thought about this a lot. This crystal clear light, I think, is the explanation. It gives everything a new meaning, form and structure of the landscape is defined and enlarged by it. The atmosphere is so very stimulating, savage, strong, primitive, beautiful . . . it's all these and much more besides. Words are really inadequate. The most important part, to me, is this mysterious X, an artist must *feel* about a place to paint it and be true to his art. Light, atmosphere, shimmering of pale, bleached grasses, surging half seen rocks, mist, rain, storm and sun on moors and headlands and, of course, skies, skies and skies . . . this is part of what I try to paint.

I'm primarily a landscape painter. This, of course, is a wide term, it *can* include portraiture because a human face is also a landscape . . . but, for me, the coasts, seas, moors, skies and rocks of Cornwall offer inexhaustible painting material . . . the peculiar clarity of light which throws this landscape of West Penwith into sharp perspective. It's a land of great antiquity, primeval and sometimes savage, why, the skies, even on a hot day, hold threats of storm clouds and the clouds, by their shadows, give form to the landscape below . . . and the light shining through can give exciting effects. Turner, the greatest British painter, I think, spent most of his life painting the effects of wind, rain and storm.

There are, of course, many ways a painting can begin. It can be an idea which ties up suddenly with something seen, more often it's a logical development of a previous painting. It's not the beginning, it's often the end or the middle, when the difficulties are greatest. I draw and sketch a lot . . . literally hundreds. It might be a movement of a wave over submerged rocks or a thrusting granite headland . . . drawing lays bare the bones of the landscape for me, it's like a map into a strange country, it helps to build an image, but it can never be the complete image. One constantly rejects, selects, searches again . . . an interesting stone from the beach, a lichen twig, a piece of seaweed . . . they can all help to start the chain reaction for the beginning of a painting. . . .

Margo Maeckleberghe is one of the most exciting painters now working in Cornwall precisely because her work reflects the strange intangible way in which Cornwall, the land, the place, does in fact influence, indeed enter into the artist. In her landscapes the Cornish imagery is so vital and striking that it almost seems to come alive before your eyes—a line of thought enhanced by her most recent series of Atlantic paintings, in which slices of Cornish landscape and coastline merge mysteriously into the shape of a reclining woman.

Interestingly, another woman painter, Misomè Peile of St Ives, underlined a similar point when she once confessed that she gave up drawing for three years to learn to think and feel only the painted surface. Hundreds of action-drawings of the wilderness of Carbis Bay, close to her studio, enabled her to break through to the fusion of sky, land and water under the brilliant hillside light—now she sees the human form in all landscape and in the heavens.

It is not without significance that so many abstract artists have been drawn to Cornwall (and rather amusing that because the landscape is so impressive not even the abstract artists have been able to keep it out of their work). I recall some interesting remarks on this point by the late Charles Marriott, one-time art critic of THE TIMES, in suggesting that West Cornwall was in particular a draughtsman's country:

Seen from a height such as Trencrom or Carn Galve the landscape runs to a decorative pattern; a sort of *cloisonné* effect of little green fields inset in a network of gorse-clad hedges. I have a notion that even in their abstractions painters such as Ben Nicholson get nearer to the peculiar magic of West Cornwall than did the painters of my day.

The painters of Charles Marriott's day, of course, were such formidable figures, often RA's, as Sir Alfred Munnings, Stanhope Forbes, Laura Knight, John Park, Lamorna Birch. . . . These were all artists of great professional skill, many of whom—notably Stanhope Forbes, with his vast canvases of Cornish fishing-life, or John Park with his tranquil oils of country views—provided a valuable record of a Cornwall that is fast disappearing. In general it is difficult to find coherent expression by traditional painters of what made them come to work in Cornwall, but fortunately Stanhope Forbes once wrote an article for Sir Arthur Quiller-Couch's CORNISH MAGAZINE, in which he looked back on the early days of the 1800's, when he and his fellow artists first descended in large numbers on the simple fishing folk of Newlyn and St Ives.

Those were the days of unflinching realism, of the cult of Bastien Lepagé. It was part of our artistic creed to paint our pictures direct from Nature, and not merely to rely upon sketches and studies which we could afterwards amplify in the comfort of a studio. It is a debatable practice, and this is not the place to argue such technicalities, but I mention it because, being strongly held by many of us, it imparted a noticable feature to local life. Artists are common enough objects by the seaside; but it was scarcely so usual to see the painter not merely engaged upon a small sketch or panel, but with a large canvas securely fastened to some convenient boulder, absorbed in the very work with which he hoped to win fame in the ensuing spring; perhaps even the model posing in full view of the entire populace, the portrait being executed with a publicity calculated to unnerve even our practised brother of the pavement.

Stanhope Forbes and his fellow artists (regarded as 'revolutionaries' in their time) painted the Cornwall they saw with their own eyes. Ben Nicholson and many other abstract painters who followed him down to Cornwall took a very different viewpoint. This has been expressed rather well, I think, by John Wells of Newlyn:

So all around the morning air and the sea's blue light with points of diamond and the gorse incandescent beyond the trees; countless rocks, ragged or round and of every colour; birds resting or flying and the sense of a multitude of creatures living out their minute lives. All this is part of one's life and I was desperately eager to express it; not just what I see, but what I feel about it and beyond it . . . But how can one paint the warmth of the sun, the sound of the sea, the journey of a beetle across a rock, or thoughts of one's own whence and whither? That's one argument for abstraction. One absorbs all these feelings and ideas; if one is lucky they undergo an alchemistic transformation into gold and that is the creative work.

Ben Nicholson, who came to live in Cornwall in 1939 and spent the next 20 years in his adopted county, has expounded further on the abstract artist's outlook. He sees painting and religious experience as the same thing, a search for the understanding and realisation of infinity—an idea that is complete with no beginning, no end, and therefore giving to all things for all time. The structure of Cornwall, he confessed, suited him ideally,

I want to be so free that I even would not need to use free colour. I dislike the idea that a picture is something precious, the painter something special. There is an artist in everybody. That was the reason why I welcomed the technique of COLLAGE. One discovers new things. One does not paint only in one medium, it does away with the precious quality of the easel picture. Art is work and play for me. And work and play are as necessary for me as breathing.

Yesterday I began to paint the garden gate. As soon as my hand touches a brush, my imagination begins to work. When I finished I went up to my studio and made a picture. Can you imagine the excitement which a line gives you when you draw it across a surface? It is like walking through the country from St Ives to Zennor . . .

Anyone who knows Cornwall, who has perhaps indeed walked through the country from St Ives to Zennor, will know what Ben Nicholson means. Abstract painting comes from looking at the sea, the land, the sky; it is visual experience, it couldn't be anything else—one is what one has seen.

Another 'foreign' abstract painter who came and settled in Cornwall for many years, Terry Frost, expounded further on this theme:

I recently completed a Blue Movement painting. I had spent a number of evenings looking out over the harbour at St Ives in Cornwall. Although I had been observing a multiplicity of movement during these evenings they all evolved a common emotion or mood—a state of delight in front of nature. On one particular blue twilit evening I was watching what I can only describe as a synthesis of movement and counter movement. That is to say, the rise and fall of the boats, the space drawings of the mastheads, the opposing movements of the incoming sea and the outblowing offshore wind—all this plus the predominant feel of blue in the evening and the static brown of the foreshore generated an emotional state which was to find expression in the painting. . . . It was not portraying the boats, the sand, the horizon or any other subject matter, but concentrating on the emotion engendered by what I saw. The subject matter is in fact the sensation evoked by the movements and the colour in the harbour. What I painted was an arrangement of form and colour which evokes for me a similar feeling.

It is perhaps not surprising that sculptors, in particular, have been most profoundly influenced—one might even say uplifted—by Cornwall. This is especially so today; but there was one Cornish sculptor who made his mark in the early nineteenth century, whose work has been marvellously commemorated in a poem by Charles Causley, 'Nevill Northey Burnard' (partly reproduced in the chapter on poets). Causley paints a vivid picture of the sculptor working away at the moorstone until at last he 'quietly lifted out his prize of rock'. Every sculptor who comes to Cornwall is confronted with this exciting chance of lifting out his 'prize of rock'—more so, surely, than in any other part of Britain. For Cornwall is the land of granite, the land whose agelessness is somehow symbolised in that very stone.

This is truly a sculptor's country, itself made of granite, but few have realised it. The terraced landscape of the little fishing towns and the geological nature of the rock at once become operative, along with the submarine cargo of shells, skulls, fish and plants, in orientating one's vision back to the fundamental shape of nature as was the case with the sculptors of earlier civilisations.

So wrote Sven Berlin, a well known sculptor who lived and worked for many years on the Island at St Ives—a colourful figure with his huge frame, bearded face crowned with an old seaman's hat, daily to be seen working in his yard hewing away at huge lumps of alabaster and blue stone. He went on to describe the excitement he felt when the Cornish sea 'got into' a shape he was carving, how 'it goes charging through the whole of the stone and the man, as if by magic, is transformed into an ocean with rocks and tides, shells and caves—a sea dragon.' It was Cornwall, Sven Berlin found, that helped to release and develop his ability to create living things in stone, the stone being an entity in itself, with a centre of vitality and tension that could be made to exist in space.

At one stage he found himself so deeply rooted in the Cornish landscape he felt quite sure that to go and carve in a different environment would completely alter his vision and approach. No doubt he little imagined himself ever leaving Cornwall then, but in fact many years later he did move to the New Forest, and his work did alter very considerably. Significantly, though, he has never been able to forget his Cornish experience, and indeed it proved so strong as to impel him to express it very successfully through another art form—the novel (anyone who wants to capture a most penetrating interpretation of Cornwall should read that novel, *The Dark Monarch*). It isn't always that one comes upon an artist in one field, in this case sculpture, who happens to be really fluent in another; and it is instructive, indeed, to quote these reflections from Sven Berlin upon Cornwall's influence on his creative work;

The open coliseum of each little cover of sand or rock may be the theatre for any natural, supernatural or unnatural event. The unending presence of the sea breathing ceaselessly over the shoulder of each hill, the rock changed with a thousand sunsets or carved by a hundred years of rain, the little trees loaded with berries growing away from the prevailing wind, offering crimson to green, the mind's incessant vertigo at the cliff edge, and the slow constructional flight of the seagull—these things in some way act as the charming of magicians and open up the deeper rooms of experience of man, making him aware of his being part of the natural universe, at the head of a great unseen procession of gods and devils, spectres and dragons; of being a channel for unknown and undefined forces; of facing the mysteries of life, awakening powers of perception which search beyond the frontiers of normal events.

That extract comes from Berlin's book on Alfred Wallis, the old St Ives fisherman turned primitive painter who at the age of 70 began painting in housepaint on old pieces of cardboard, a flood of child-like efforts which today are on the walls of numerous art galleries and treasured in many private collections. At first sight many of Wallis's paintings do, indeed, seem like the sort of pictures pinned up on classroom walls in infant schools; but on closer inspection one begins to have second thoughts (especially in his last terrifying Death Ship paintings). The fact is that this gnarled, turned-in, suspicious, pernickety old Cornishman was impelled to give creative expression to what was there, in his own land—just as outsiders of intuition, like Berlin, coming to live there, had a similar reaction.

Wallis is not the only primitive painter of Cornwall. Jack Pender's grandfather, W.J.George, another fisherman, also started painting in his old age, producing hundreds of canvases from the age of 75 until his death at 94. One of these was described by his grandson like this, 'Three black boats, brown mizzen sails steadying, white foam creaming their bows, hurrying to Newlyn fish market. Past the granite and white cottage homes of their crews, past the reaching arms of their home harbour, past the protecting island that forms a natural breakwater to the one time busy fishing village of Mousehole. The urgency of their progress is witnessed, felt, recorded.'

'Witnessed, felt, recorded'—that is what every painter of any stature who works in Cornwall seems somehow to be compelled to follow. It can be seen in the primitive work of Wallis or George, or Mary Jewells of Newlyn, or Bryan Pearce of St Ives (a courageous figure suffering from *phynylktenuea*, a rare disease that retards mental progress, who nevertheless has produced armfuls of fascinating studies of Cornish towns and landscapes seen through his extraordinarily perceptive eye). In the works of the simple primitive artist is reflected more starkly and directly exactly the same thing that is to be found in the less simple work of abstract painters such as Ben Nicholson or John Wells, or in the sculpture of Sven Berlin—or of that internationally famous sculptor Barbara Hepworth, who in her studio at Trewyn, St Ives, has produced a series of masterpieces now exhibited all over the world. As one art critic rightly commented, Barbara Hepworth is deeply under the influence of Cornwall because that landscape, perhaps more than any other, must call up a deep emotional response from an artist so much of whose life is concerned with digging deep into the heart of her materials and searching out basic forms.

Go into any art gallery in Cornwall—whether the more sophisticated galleries of the Penwith Society at St Ives or the Newlyn Society at Newlyn, or the smaller galleries to be found in Polperro, Looe, Boscastle, Padstow, Newquay, Fowey, Falmouth—and certain interesting factors will be noted. First, by far the greatest percentage of the painters exhibiting will be non-Cornish—i.e. artists who have been drawn to Cornwall, have settled here to work. Second, the variety of their work, and that of their Cornish companions, will be quite remarkable, ranging from traditional to pop, from figurative to abstract, from landscapes to geometrical formations. Thirdly, and this is the really significant factor, with the single obvious exception of portraiture, it is almost certain that every single painting or sculpture will somehow reflect that Cornish environment out of which it has been created.

That environment is difficult to pin down directly. Of course, from a superficial point of view there are many obvious aspects of very definite importance in their own way. For instance, from the sheerly economical view, painter's studios are not to be found growing on trees—in most parts of Britain they would be an unusual feature indeed, but in Cornwall they are, in fact, reasonably plentiful. St Ives is perhaps something of a special case, but it is worth noting that in this small fishing-town alone there are probably upwards of 50 professional artists' studios, all occupied by working artists (some of them, like Porthmeor and the former Piazza Studios set, overlooking one of the most beautiful beaches in Britain). Similarly in Newlyn, in Mousehole, Penzance and surrounding areas, artists' studios are to be found in comparative profusion, often custom built, but equally often converted successfully from former barns or even cowsheds. Where there's a will, there has to be a way. The same can be said for many other areas: Polperro, Fowey, Looe, Falmouth, Truro, Tintagel, Boscastle, Wadebridge. Indeed the artist's studio in Cornwall is almost as commonplace as, say, a pottery in Stoke (though even here, as is indicated in the crafts chapter, Cornwall can boast more potteries than any other English county).

In such a background, allied to the multiplicity of art societies and artists' clubs—and even such socially encouraging facts as numerous and attractive pubs where artists can meet for convivial evenings—it is only to be expected that painters feel an empathy, an encouragement to work. Yet when all this is admitted, there remains something further to be said: something that can hardly be put directly, but is most effective when hinted at almost ambiguously, as in a piece which the late Peter Lanyon once wrote for me for the CORNISH REVIEW. It was called 'The Face of Penwith' and I feel it makes a fitting finale to this chapter:

The Cornishman is not double-faced but multiple-faced, facets of character which add up to a sort of innocence. He is never still himself except in death, but all the conflicts which lead to a game of hide and seek between native and the so-called 'foreigner' are part of a process which constantly surfaces the most diverse and conflicting factors. The Cornishman is fond of private secrets. A solemn intercourse of native with native, often intimate, is mistaken for a gossiping and vicious moralizing. The bush telegraph which puts the G.P.O. to shame is a part of this intimate revelation from native to native. The part of this game which is revealed to the unfortunate 'foreigner' is that part which concerns him alone, the rest is none of his business. Prayer is a strong force, and in the greatest days of revivalist services, in Wesleyan chapels, a poetic resolution was achieved. The loss of such inspiring services is as sad for Cornwall as the closing of the mines.

There is a main force which is centrifugal and centripetal, a giving out and a taking in. In extremes this means a complete trust and desire to give absolutely everything and a converse withdrawal, a returning to a protective native envelope. The eye is prospecting and adventurous, it has also an inward look. Perhaps these qualities are most often found in insular people, and perhaps Cornwall itself has for centuries been almost an island. The intimate contacts of native with native revealed in CORNISH STORIES (understood and enjoyed for their peculiar flavour by natives only) remains. The Cornishman will change according to basic rhythms which are suggested here and will make a good job a 'fitty' job, as he says, not one just fit for purpose but a fitness within a rightness which is determined by his whole history and the nature of his country.

The following sketches offer suggestions towards a revelatory process. They are made from outside by a certain detachment which is the artists' method, but from within also, in the hope that processes of revelation, extension and creation (latent in familiar objects) may themselves be revealed and shown to have a relativity in time and space. This complication of a familiar and plain scene is made in the interests of an analysis of Cornish character. In the congregation of the Cornish cross, a circular theme, the symbol of this process stands erect, revealed and outward, in the landscape.

1. LANDSCAPE

From Wicca to Levant the coastline emerges out of carns and bracken and cultivated greenland, revealing on its varied faces a sea history and a land history of men within and without and a commerce of man with the weather. Here, in a small stretch of headland, cove and Atlantic adventure, the most distant histories are near the surface as if the final convulsion of rock upheaval and cold incision, setting in a violent sandwich of strata, had directed the hide and seek of Celtic pattern. A motor-boat in some solemn gaiety with insistent cough, searches out the exacted payment of ocean on land; the small ritual of business at the junction of rock and sea wall.

On carns of Zennor, Hannibal and Galva, where giants may have hurled their googlies in mild recreation, an outline of earthwork makes evidence for a primitive brotherhood of man, of the great and small in life and death wherein animal joy and terror found resolution in the protective care

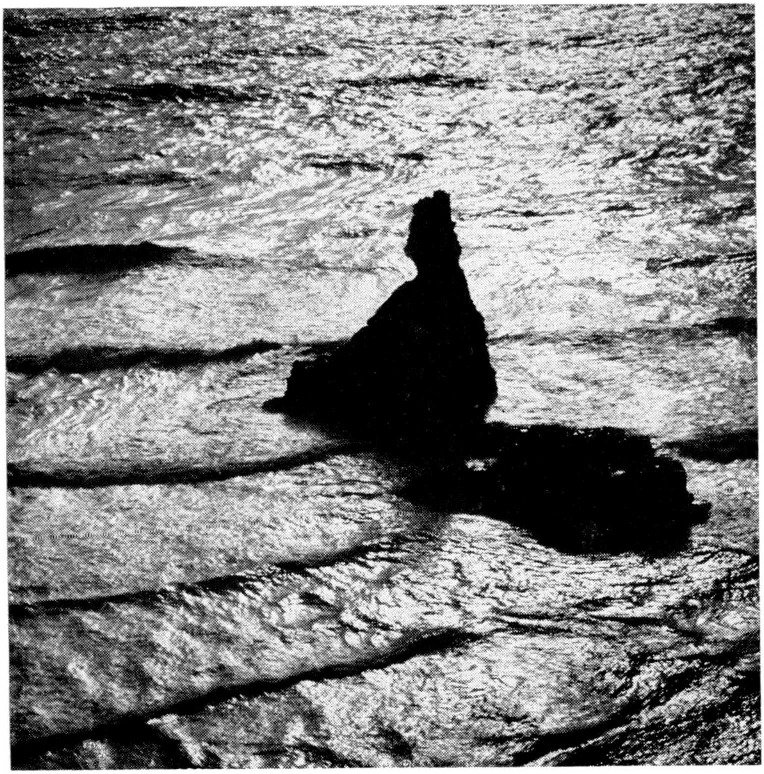

1 Queen Bess Rock

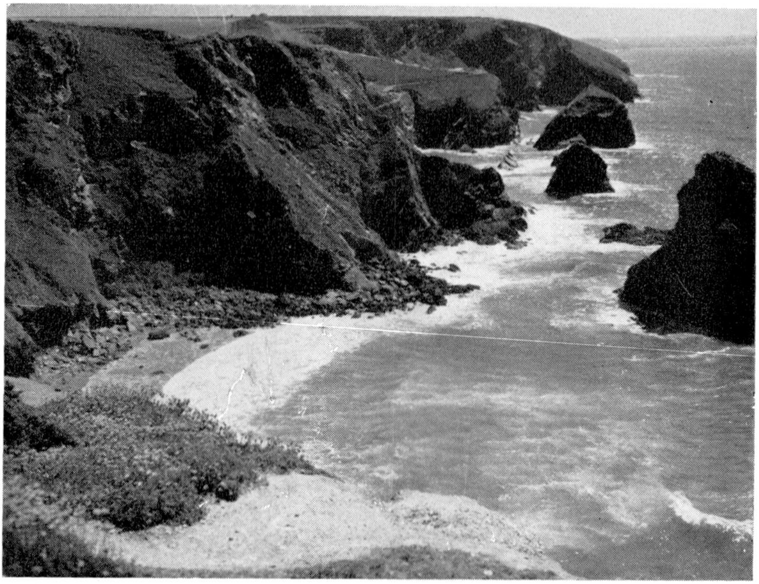

2 Bedruthan Steps

3 Puffins

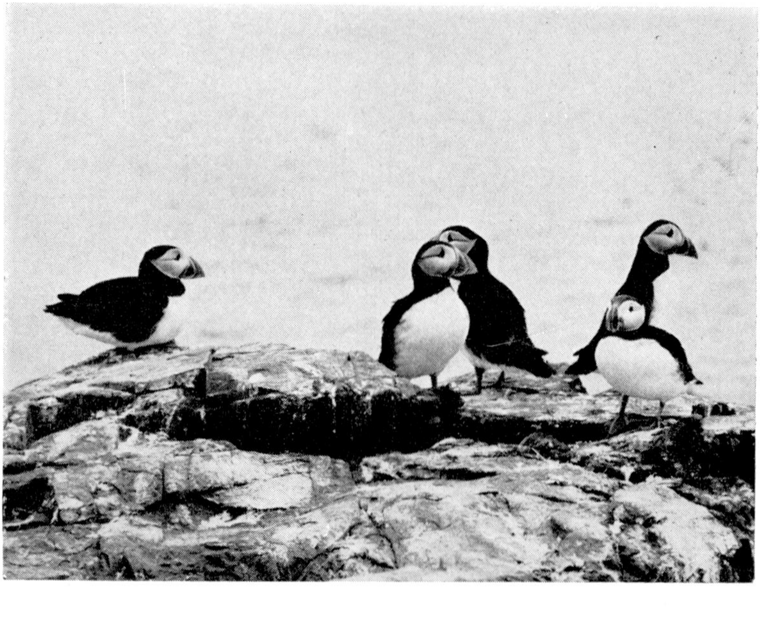

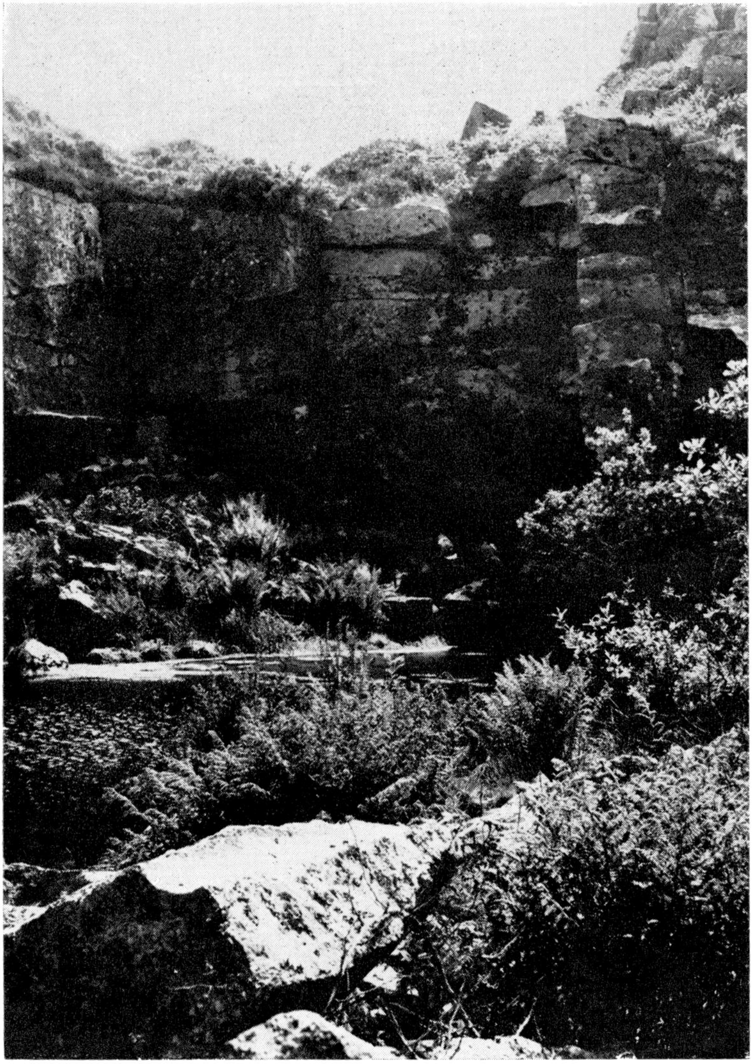

4 Cornish Quarry

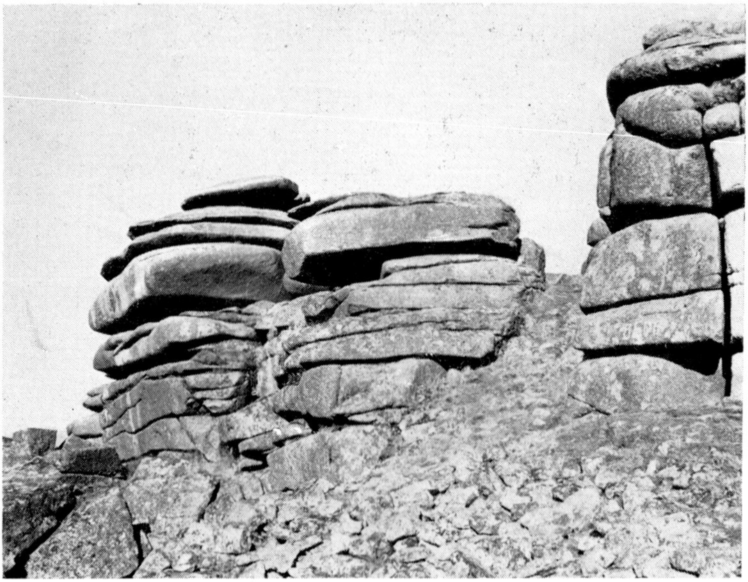

5 Bodmin Moor (see p. 39)

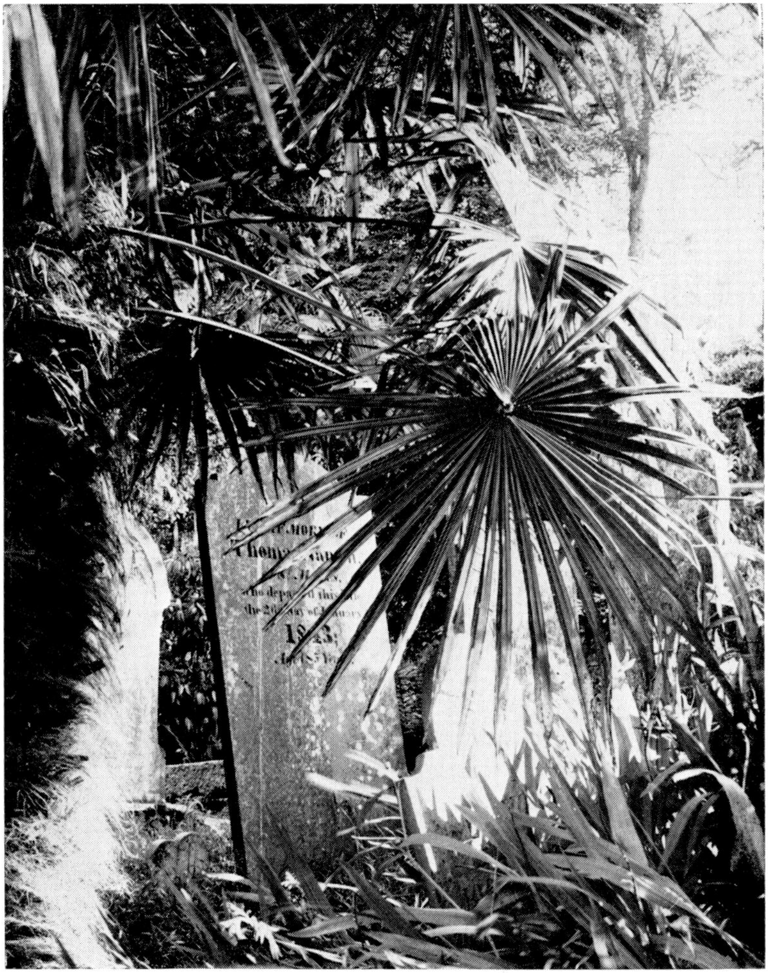

6 St Just in Roseland Churchyard

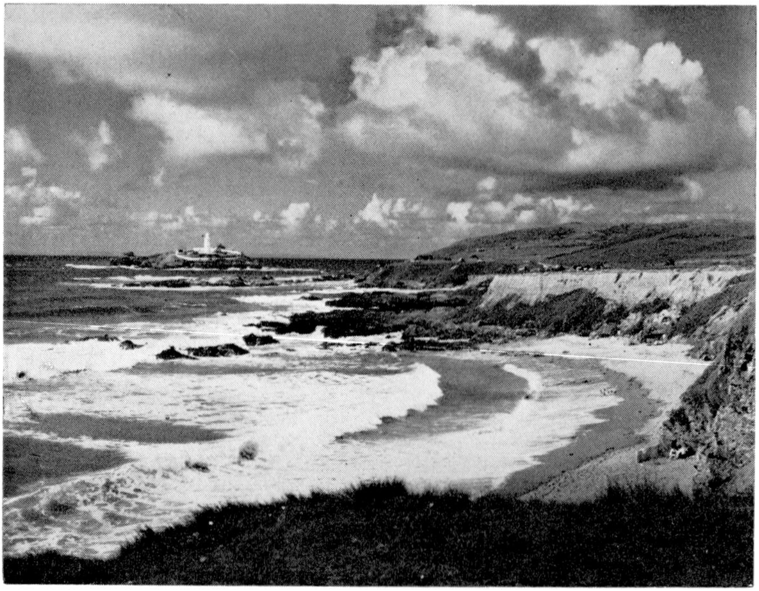

7 Godrevy

8 China Clay Works (see p. 71)

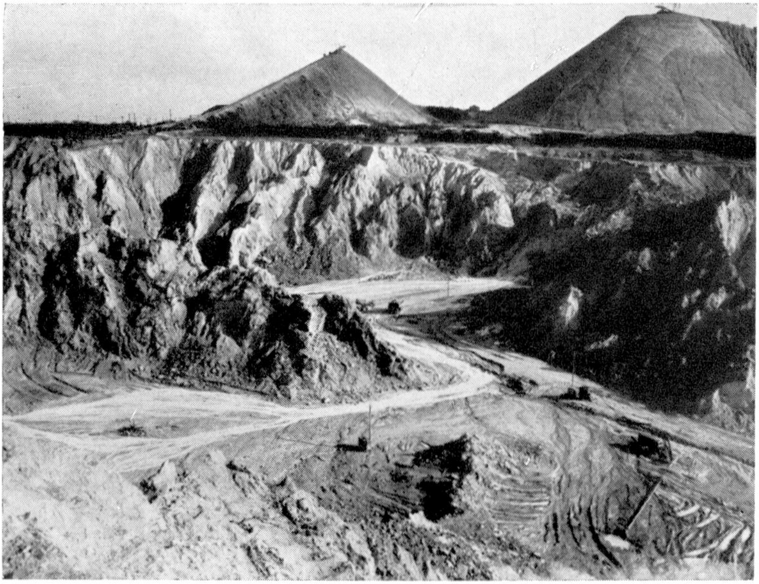

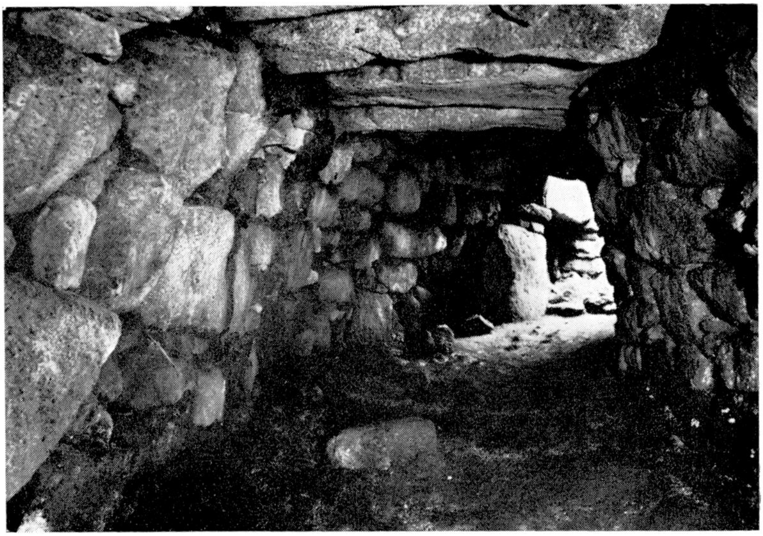

9 Carn Euny Fogue

10 Merry Maidens

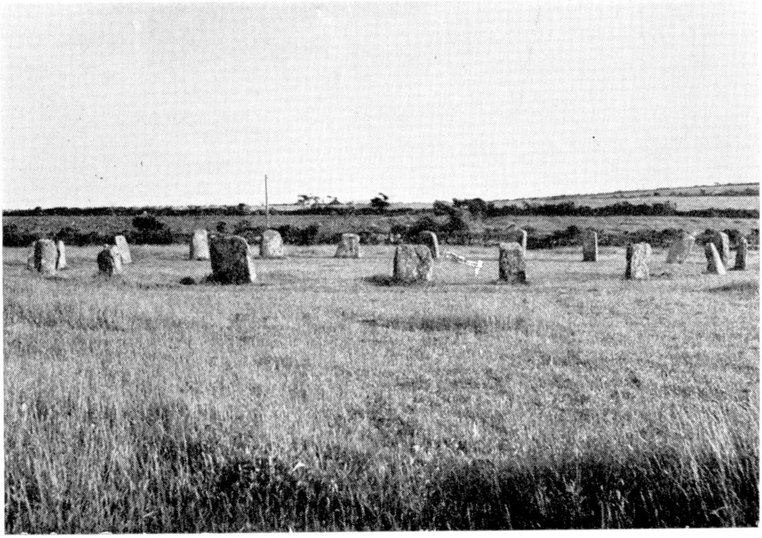

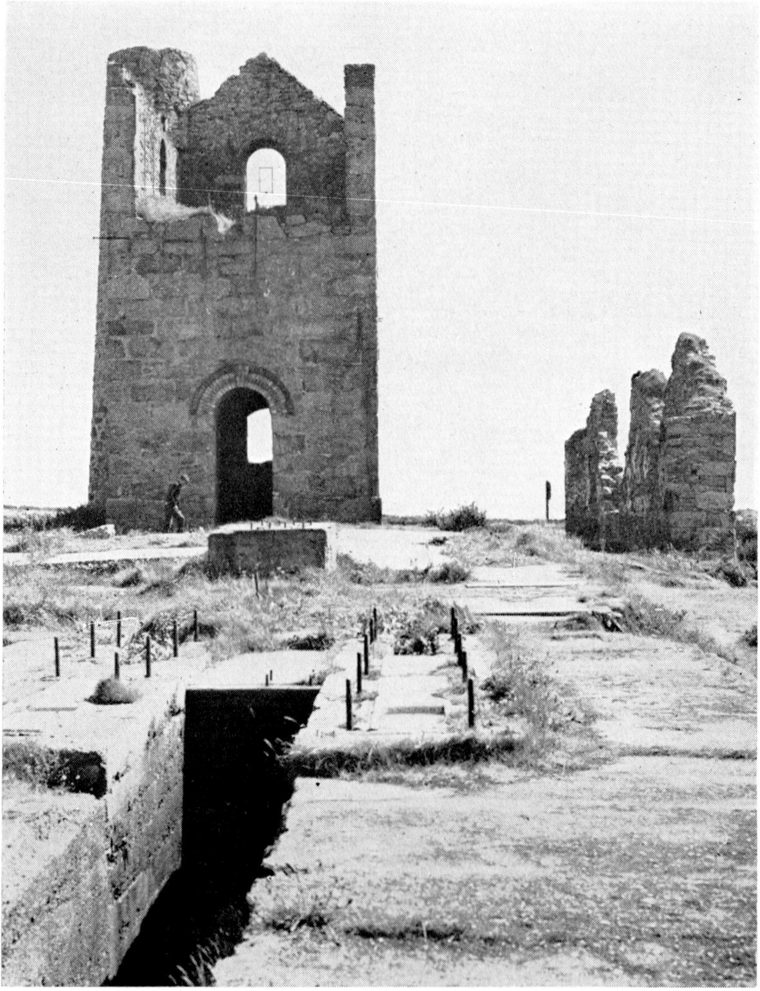

11 Old Tin Mine, St Ives

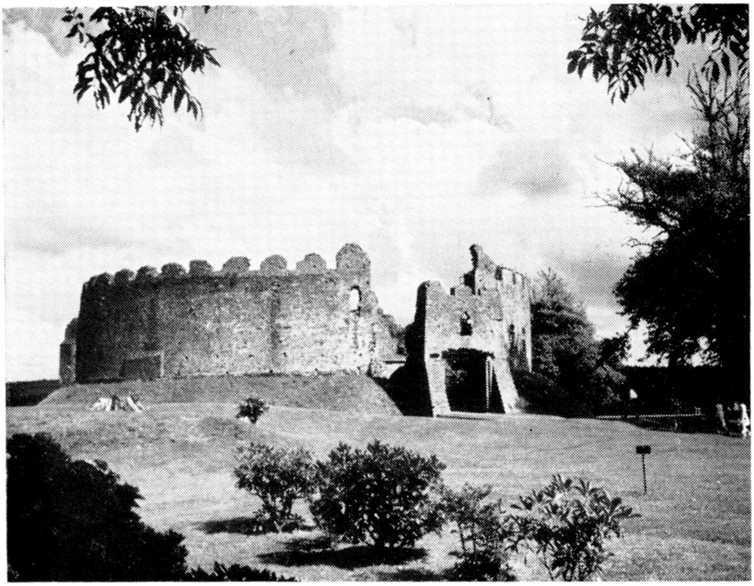

12 Restormel Castle (see p. 57)

13 Blue Hills, St Agnes

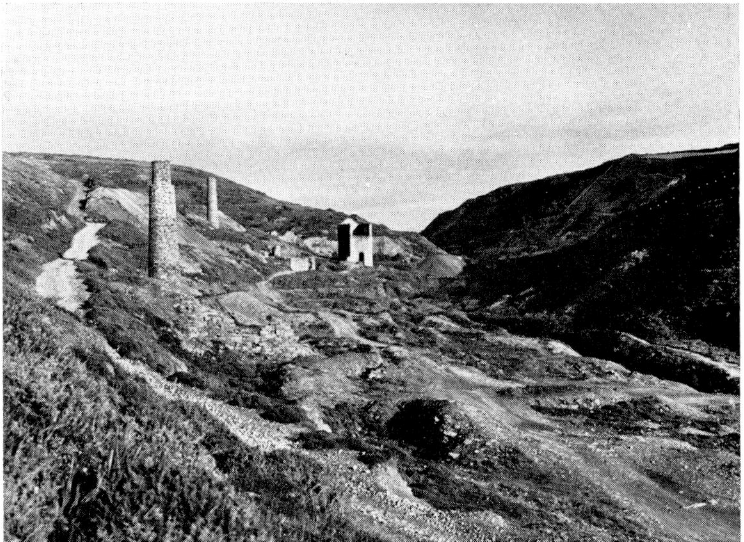

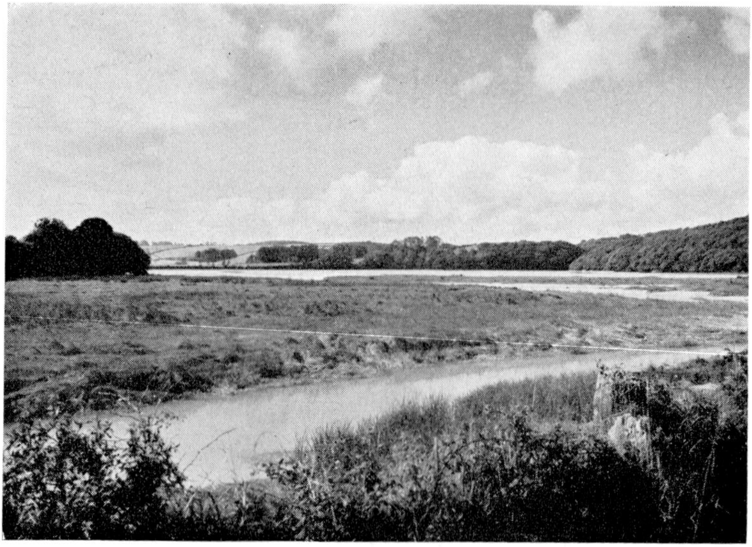

14 Ruan Lanhorne

15 Bodmin Moor (see p. 11)

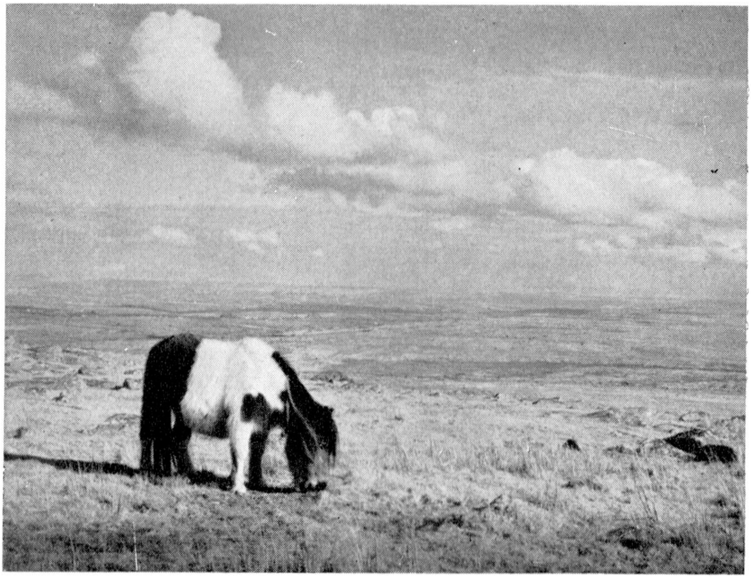

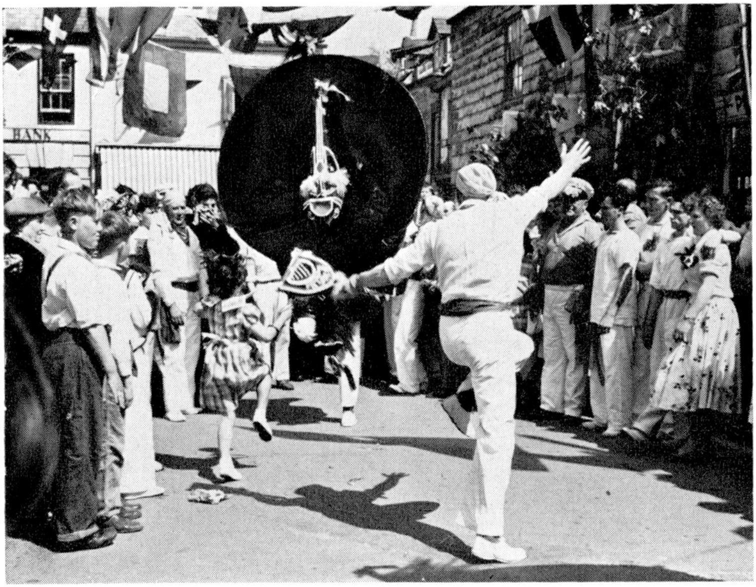

16 Padstow Hobby Horse (see p. 53)

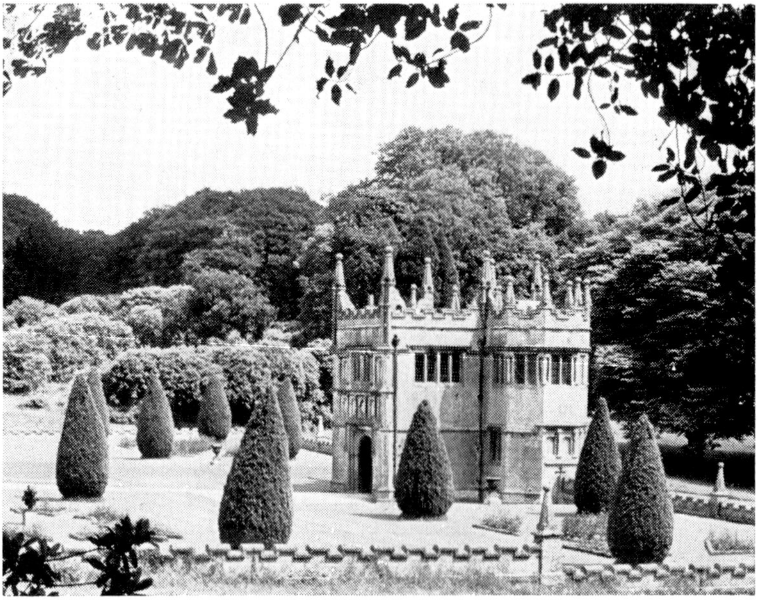

17 Lanydrock House Gatehouse

18 St Just Church

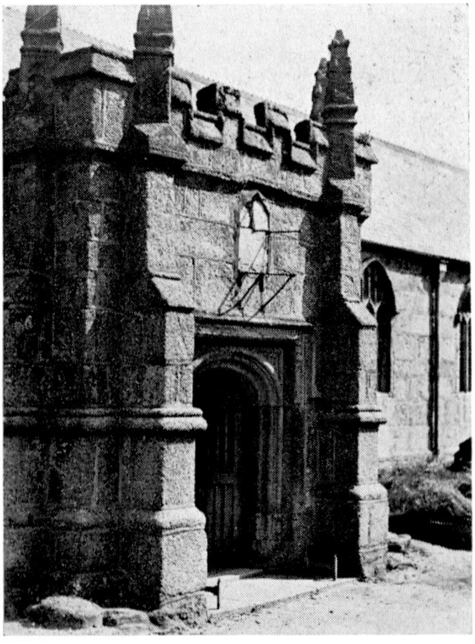

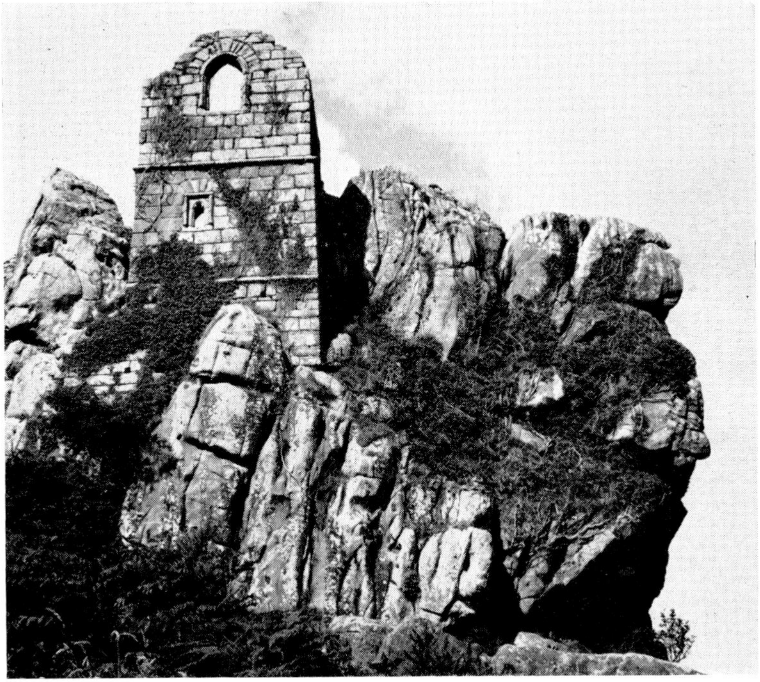

19 Roche Hermitage

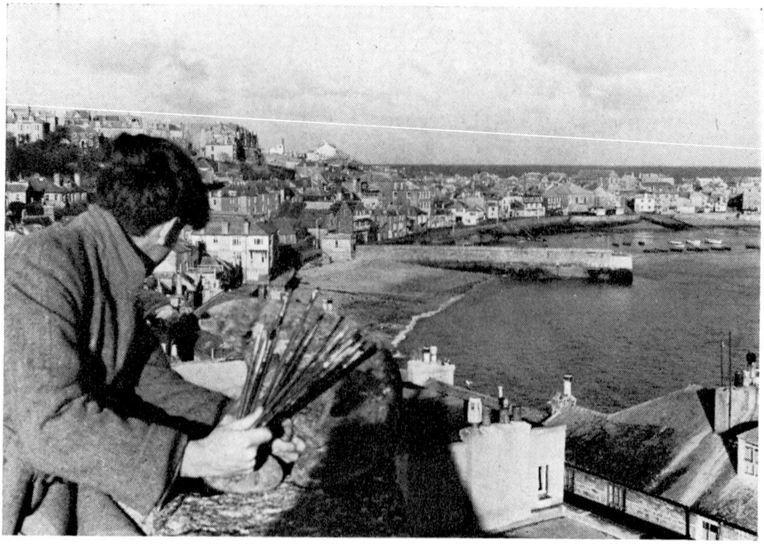

20 St Ives (see p. 14)

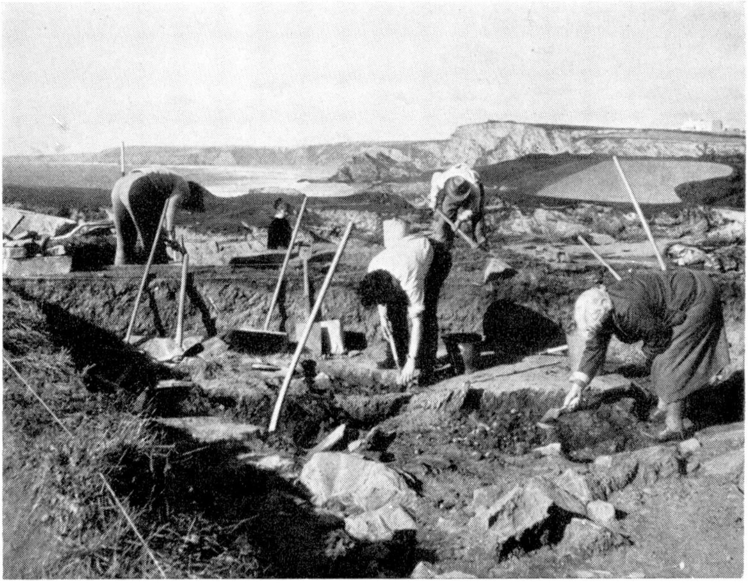

21 Glendorgal Dig (Charles Woolf)

22 Perran Round, St Just (see p. 52)

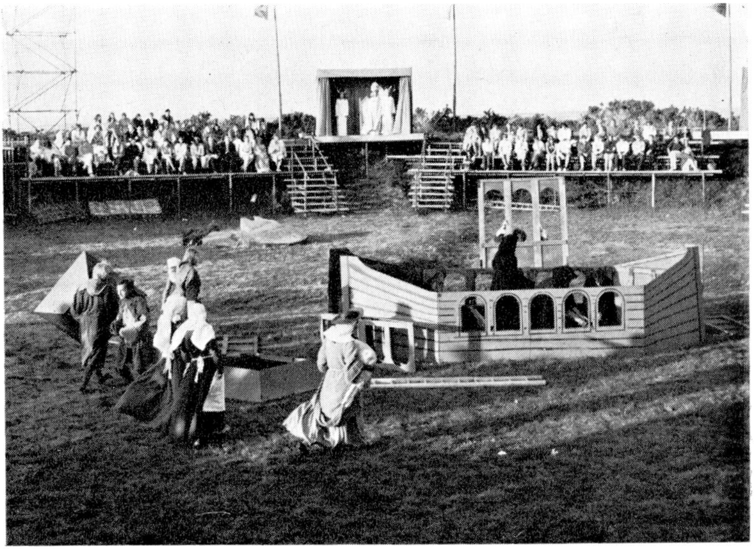

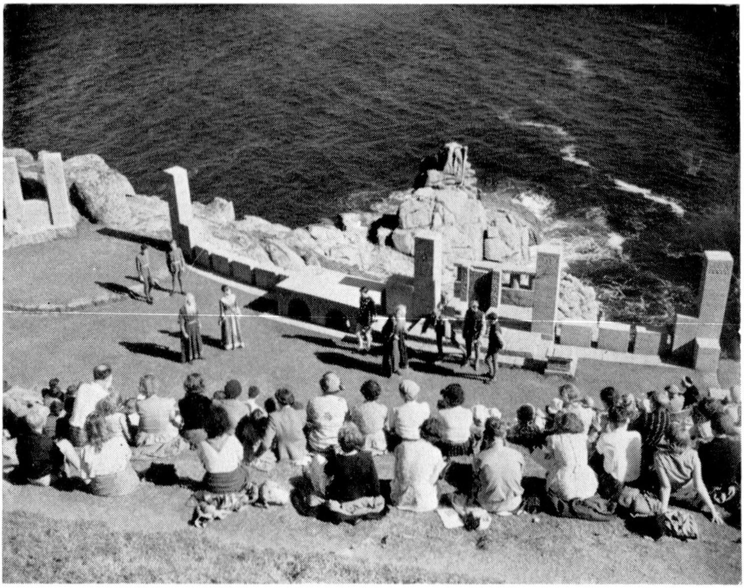

23, 24 The Minack Theatre (see pp. 55 and 56)

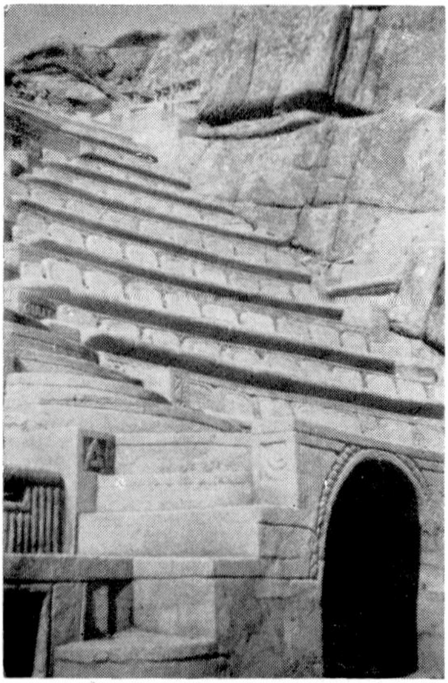

of monolith and fort. Hereabouts, perhaps, the sun set westwards, shifting down the monolith to bury the light of primitive fire, and rose again in the hearts of men from the east. The saints were in Cornwall.

From Levant to Wicca, an easterly direction, chimneys are crowned by brick flourish and the towers are lichen-covered, castellated and pinnacled. They rise upward out of the horizontal ground as if the thrust of stone had surfaced to the call of the native, given up its wealth to his endeavour, and been revealed by manufacture as an expression of inner intent. Invention, leading to extension of native culture, made present in time a process of ancient developments. The craft and skill and meaning of the native journey are outward and revealed at the land surface.

2. VOYAGES OF THE NATIVE

To bring the world within the hand and make immediate the farthest shore, seamen set sail for the mistress of the sea. From storm and shipwreck the homing seaman returns with cargo, unloading on granite quays a wealth of image. What stories he tells, and in his sea soul gives to the land, remain outwardly in his artefacts, are revealed to generations by the face of man and the character of his seaborn gear. This process has been a source of man's struggle to make himself as outward and revealed as this place of granite. Here sea and land answer the deep roots of man and present him with a face.

At Levant Mine, where tin and ocean meet, men fished for food after labour beneath the ocean bed. What is within the granite arms of harbour, sheltered from surface mood and ground sea is concerned with an intimate bobbing, the playful game of boat with mooring, a small outward exchange reflective of deep ocean movements. A happy commerce in granite embrace. But the centre and focus of lighthouse, port and parent are left alone as masts and sails, clumsy with their clawings, move out to their own aggressiveness. Man-engine and steam haulage pass contact to deep levels with man-baited rod and line. Where shifts go down and come up and ships in regular exchange remove themselves and return to parent, the resources of Cornwall are best displayed and landed. In every small and intimate departure or arrival a wholeness of living is revealed, and in commerce of man with granite and Atlantic the transitory is made immediate, each facet being related elementally to the next as aspect and image of a whole.

3. JOURNEY OF THE VISITOR

Running along Hayle estuary and round points to St Ives terminus a local train brings the man from pavement, office and city statue to a most complete revelation of history in the earth, to the open face of his country, the ultimate and prized beauty of the flower.

Richard Trevithick made a steam engine, a concoction of homely kettle and manufacture, a concept of extension whereby man's muscled arm is replaced by an idea made solid, of motion and power in simple movements. Steam expansion and piston, valve gear and con rod, cranked for transference to rotary motion; the divider and compass, straight line and circle, all set on the wheels of a horseless cart for the ride up Camborne hill in glory.

The industrial revolution moved inward and outward down and up the line: Par, Lostwithiel, Truro, Redruth, Camborne, Truro, St Austell and Saltash. From within the drawbridge fell across the Tamar.

To the demands of extension the Cornishman, evolving his time theme, the centrifugal and the centripetal, makes invention, making real the face of his own time, making object and image from within.

IV

Poets'-eye View

ALTHOUGH the fact tends to be less publicized, poets have been drawn to Cornwall just as numerously as painters. When we search back into history and find the great landscape-painter Turner touring Cornwall and quickly filling his sketchbook, we can soon match that by discovering that none other than Alfred Lord Tennyson, the Poet Laureate himself, once spent a summer holiday tramping around Cornwall, averaging 10 miles a day and keeping a diary of visits to such spots as King Arthur's Castle at Tintagel. The diary is full of vivid phrases such as 'glorious grass-green monsters of waves', and 'when the long wave broke all down the thundering shores of Bude and Boss, there came a day as still as heaven.' Certainly it is not difficult to trace much of the imagery of Tennyson's later epic poems to that summer-time wandering along the North Coast—Bude, Boscastle, Tintagel, Camelford—and later on, the South Coast, Penzance, Marazion, St Michael's Mount, Falmouth—always in sight of the sea . . .

> After the sunset, down the coast he heard
> Strange music, and he paused and turning—there,
> All down the lonely coast of Lyonesse,
> Each with a beacon star upon his head,
> And with a wild sea-light about his feet,
> He saw them—headland after headland flame
> Far on into the rich heart of the west.

Another great English writer of the nineteenth century, though best known as a novelist, found unusual poetic fulfilment in Cornwall—Thomas Hardy. When only 29 and a struggling young architect, he was invited to St Juliot's Rectory, Boscastle, to make a report on proposed renovations. The rector's sister-in-law Emma, acted as hostess, and Hardy immediately fell in love with her. Forty years afterwards he sat down and remembered the event in a poem which began:

> When I set out for Lyonesse,
> A hundred miles away,
> The rime was on the spray,

And starlight lit my lonesomness,
When I set out for Lyonesse
A hundred miles away.

and the poem concludes triumphantly:

When I came back from Lyonesse
With magic in my eyes,
All marked with mute surmise
My radiance rare and fathomless,
When I came back from Lyonesse,
With magic in my eyes!

Thomas Hardy married Emma, and though the marriage later turned sour, after her death in 1912 his mind turned back to those romantic early days, and he returned on a pilgrimage to Cornwall. Out of that visit—made long after he had given up writing novels—were born some of the most moving and passionate love poems in the English language, almost all of them directly connected with Cornwall. Indeed, Cornwall must have sunk deeply into the writer's consciousness, for almost every poem captures an atmosphere peculiar only to this county. Here for instance are some lines set on Beeny Cliff at Boscastle:

O the opal and the sapphire of that wandering western sea,
And the woman riding high above with bright hair flapping free—
The woman whom I love so, and who loyally loved me.
The pale mews plained below us and the waves seemed far away
In a nether sky, engrossed in saying their ceaseless babbling say,
As we laughed light-heartedly aloft on that clear sunned March day.
A little cloud then cloaked us, and there flew an irised rain,
And the Atlantic dyed its levels with a dull misfeatured stain,
And then the sun burst out again and purples prinked the main.

What a marvellous opening line—and how accurately it captures all the mystery and magic associated with Cornwall! Here again we see how such a strange and surely unique background stimulates the artist continually. In Hardy's *Collected Poems* there are not just one or two, but dozens of poems that continually surprise by their freshness and vividness.

Beeny did not quiver,
Juliot grew not grey,
Thin Vallency's river
Held its wonted way.
Bos seemed not to utter
Dimmest note of dirge
Targen mouth a mutter
To its creamy surge.

Uniquely Cornish places like Beeny Cliff seemed perpetually to draw Hardy's interest:

> What if still in chasmal beauty looms that wild weird western shore,
> The woman now is—elsewhere—whom that ambling pony bore,
> And nor knows nor cares for Beeny, and will laugh there never more.

Writing of the way in which Cornwall cast its spell on Thomas Hardy's works, particularly his poetry, the critic Elizabeth Beard once commented that these works could be seen to owe a great deal to the especial spiritual quality of Cornwall's hard, silent, indifferent heights, with the lonely buzzard circling above and immense distance all round, with violets hidden in grassy walls and thrift growing out of the very granite . . .

> Had it been another county might these works not only have been different but also less good? It is true that the especial quality is always to some extent possessed by all high lonely coasts but not to the extent that Cornwall possesses it. It is the sense that all the things usually considered important are swept away and are not after all very important. You feel it in the great expanse of sky, sea and land. More, the sense that something else is very important if only one could grasp what. The country with its heightened strenuous bare feeling that drives one inwards to this other important thing engenders the desire for a more spacious, generous and purposive mode of life. There is something in the bareness of Cornwall that strips one of inessentials, something in the beauty of its contrasts of frail falls of pale ribbon-like water, flowering tide edges and stretches of flowers in deep valleys against the bare silent rock-like structure of its heights that puts you in touch with the desire for more everlasting beauty within civilisation.
>
> Something in rocks jutting through bare treeless soil that is akin to spiritual roots . . . Perhaps this is why Cornwall appeals to the modern artist, trapped as he is in a confusing conflict of new scientific knowledge and puzzled by the selfish structure of society and by wars he can do nothing to prevent. With such a dark philosophy it is not unlikely that Thomas Hardy is to be numbered among the many artists who had a special regard for Cornwall, the county of his romance, with its quality of sweeping away all that is usual. The lyrics surely owe something not only to Hardy and to circumstances, but also to the especial flavour of Cornwall, even suppose its beauty of form and colour alone were insufficient for such an observer of country loveliness. One could speculate that, emphasised by his wife's death, and by the temperamental estrangement of their later years, by the fact that he was himself an artist at odds with civilisation, the scene of his early romance could not have been more perfectly found than in Cornwall, with its heightened beauty and its tendency to engender spiritual introspection. The fundamental quality of the land fitted the fundamental quality of the experience recorded, and the quality of an artist in this particular age.

Tennyson and Hardy are only two of many famous poets of the past who came, saw and were conquered by mysterious Cornwall. It would be possible to produce just as impressive a catalogue as for painters, and to show how in many cases the influence of the county upon the poets was so strong as to draw them back again and again, even sometimes taking up permanent residence, as John Davidson did in Penzance. There have been remarkable Cornish-born poets of the past, too—men like John Harris, the poet-miner of Camborne who was working in Dolcoath, Cornwall's deepest tin-mine, at the age of only thirteen:

> The heat, the cold, the sulphur and the slime,
> The grinding masses of the loosened rock,
> The scaling ladders, the incessant grime
> From the dark timbers and the dripping block,
> The lassitude, the mallet's frequent knock,
> The pain of thirst when water was so near,
> The aching joints, the blasted hole's rude shock,
> Could not dash out the music from his ear,
> Or stay the sound of song which ever murmured clear.
> The cavern's sides, the vagues of shining spar,
> The roof of rock where scarce the candle gleams,
> The hollow levels strangely stretching far
> Beneath the mountains, full of mineral seams,
> Were evermore to him befitting themes,
> For meditation and his rustic lay;
> While in the darkness his pale visage gleams,
> To read rich sonnets on the furrowed clay,
> And craggy slabs that jut the ladder's lonely way.

However, it is simpler here to concentrate on examples of a more contemporary nature: and there are plenty enough of these, indeed. The poet's-eye view of Cornwall, with all its fleeting faces, has been a remarkably penetrating one, ranging from the brilliant evocation of visiting poets such as the late Dylan Thomas or John Heath-Stubbs, through the work of what might be called resident 'furriners' such as John Betjeman or the Scottish poet W.S. Graham, to native poets of the repute of A.L. Rowse, Jack Clemo and Charles Causley. Often, I think, it has been the visitor's unjaundiced and quickly emotional response which has captured most dramatically those usually hidden, or even buried elements of Cornwall. It was, for instance, John Heath-Stubbs, during a period when he shared a cottage on the cliffs at Gurnard's Head with another poet, David Wright, who wrote that vivid poem about that area beginning with the, to me, unforgettable word picture:

> This is a hideous and wicked country,
> Sloping to hateful sun sets and the end of time,
> Hollow with mine shafts, naked with granite, fanatic
> With sorrow. Abortions of the past

Hop through these bogs; black-faced the villagers
Remember burnings by the hewn stones . . .

Now a good Cornishman might take exception to the violence of some of these epithets, yet they do bring to life something which is usually left to sleep—they do remind us that not far below the surface in Cornwall there linger all kinds of strange, weird, sometimes even evil elements. We should not fear to consider such things: who knows, they may be more honest, more real, than other aspects of the more modern Cornwall—aspects paraded bitterly again by the same poet, Heath-Stubbs, in another poem, 'The Last Will and Testament of the Cornish Chough', in the CORNISH REVIEW.

Romantic Cornwall's dead and gone,
With Stephen Hawker in his tomb;
The Western Ocean breaks upon
The Land's End Point in a froth of foam—
A welter of unappeasable grief:
The artists caper in St. Ives,
Where, disembarking from his leaf,
A hermit stepped from the wild waves.
I, flame-billed Pyrrhocorax,
Guardian of King Arthur's spirit,
Croaking my last like Sycorax,
Denote to those who shall inherit:
In love of literature I grant
To That which broods upon this place—
The vision of the guarded Mount—
A footnote out of Lycidas;
To Zennor's fishy-favoured maid,
Who in her whirpool mourns alone,
By all her men unsatisfied,
Two polished orbs of Cornish stone;
To the sad-eyed Phoenician ghosts
Revisiting, in their essence thin,
Their ancient bridgeheads on these coasts,
My dangerous, derelict mines of tin;
For that notorious Queen of Cornwall,
She who with Tristan held her tryst,
What heirloom could be suitable—
Now that she's turned Methodist?
To the Bardic Gorsedd at Penwith,
And all the Olde Worlde shops,
Appropriately I bequeath
Each moulting feather as it drops;
But the royal soul of Arthur,
Crouched in my body, limb for limb—
I leave it to the British Empire,
Which certainly has need of him.

Perhaps more sympathetic to the Cornish way of life has been W.S. Graham, a Scottish-born poet who settled in West Cornwall some 20 years ago, and still lives at Madron just outside Penzance. At one time Graham was hailed as the natural successor to Dylan Thomas, and in such books as *The Night Fishermen* he certainly displayed the same amazing ability at adjectival juggling. Possibly this very romantic and lyrical poetic approach, with a vividly unexpected juxtaposition of words achieving the same effect of purpose as abstract painters in their field, does again help us to see Cornwall more clearly for what it really is. These qualities, I think, come out very clearly in a valedictory poem which Sydney Graham wrote in memory of the famous old St Ives fisherman painter, Alfred Wallis:

Worldhauled, he's grounded on God's great bank,
Keelheaved to Heaven, waved into boatfilled arms
Falls his homecoming leaving that old sea testament,
Watching the restless land sail rigged alongside
Townful of shallows, gulls on the sailing roofs.
And he's heaved once and for all a high dry packet
Pecked wide by curious years of a ferreting sea,
His poor house blessed by very poverty's religious
Breakwater, his past house hung in foreign galleries.
He's that stone sailor towering out of the cupboarding sea
To watch the black boats rigged by a question quietly
Ghost home and ask right out with jackets of oil
The standing white of the crew 'what hellward harbour
Bows down her seawalls to arriving home at last?'

Falls into home his prayer pray. He's there to lie
Seagreat and small, contrary and rare as sand
Sea sheller. Yes falls to me his kept beating, painted heart,
An ararat shore, loud limpet stuck to its terror,
Drags home the bible keel from a returning sea
And four black, shouting steerers stationed on movement
Call out arrival over the landgreat houseboat.
The ship of land with birds on seven trees
Calls out farewell like Melville talking down on
Nightfalls devoted barque and the parable whale.
What shipcry falls? The holy families of foam
Fall into wilderness and 'over the jasper sea.'
The gulls wade into silence. What deep seasaint
Whispered this keel out of its element?

Anyone reading such a poem is given a picture, in words, of what in their different ways some of the painters and sculptors have sometimes achieved in the strange formation of their materials—i.e. a vivid image of the truly subterranean nature of Cornwall and its whole way of life. This itself was indeed captured by Alfred Wallis in some of his simple yet eternally disturbing child-like paintings of Cornish fishing boats . . . and now in turn, in this fisherman memorial, Sydney Graham renews our understanding.

Another visiting poet of great sensitivity, Frances Bellerby, once wrote in a poem, 'Artist in Cornwall'

> The bones of this land are not speechless.
> So first he should learn their language,
> He whose soul, in its time-narrowed passage,
> Must mirror this place.
>
> Then, speak as he ordered
> In the clear and formal rhythm
> Of soil and rock whose wisdom
> Is the Word
>
> Made Bone; command the sea-light
> To release the pent, ingenious
> Elements; precise, fastidious,
> Sure, interpret.
>
> By arrangement, by choice. Meanwhile, blind—
> Fold, fingertip, the true veins
> Will hasten eager as fond slaves
> To chart this land
>
> By way of his own body—prove
> The plan of the Bones, the fashion
> Also of the changing Flesh, on
> His image of Love.

John Betjeman by contrast has commemorated his love for Cornwall in much lighter vein, with his nostalgic memories of childhood holidays along the North Coast at Trebetherick and Rock and Polzeath. Yet for one so well known in the more orthodox and traditional fields of poetry it is fascinating to see how persistently his muse is prodded by his Cornish experiences.

> Where yonder villa hogs the sea
> Was open cliff to you and me.
> The many-coloured caras fill
> The salty marsh to Shilla Mill
> And foreground to the hanging wood,
> Are 'toilets' where the cattle stood.

The mint and meadowsweet would scent
The brambly lane by which we went;
Now, as we near the ocean roar,
A smell of deep-fry haunts the shore.
In pools beyond the reach of tide
The Senior Service cartons glide
And on the sand the surf line lisps
With wrappings of potato crisps.
The breakers bring with merry noise
Tribute of broken plastic toys
And lichened spears of blackthorn glitter
With harvest of the August litter.
Here in the late October light
See Cornwall, a pathetic sight,
Raddled and put upon and tired
And looking somewhat over-hired,
Remembering in the autumn air
The years when she was young and fair—
Those golden and unpeopled bays,
The shadowy cliffs and sheep-worn ways,
The legions of unsurfed on surf,
The thyme and mushroom-scented turf,
The slate-hung farms, the oil-lit chapels,
Thin elms and lemon-coloured apples—
Going and gone beyond recall
Now she is free for One and All.
One day a tidal wave will break
Before the breakfasters awake
And sweep the caras out to sea
The oil the tar and you and me
And leave in windy criss cross motion
A waste of undulating ocean
From which jut out, a second Scilly,
The Isles of Roughtor and Brown Willy.

Sometimes a real foreigner, like the Polish poet Zofia Ilinska, who has lived for many years at St Mawes, where her husband runs a large hotel, brings most vividly to life an expected facet of Cornish life.

We provide the expected Pub; the Usual Barber, Baker and coffin maker
The usual female persons prepared to marry
Bearded men in charge of steamers, hooting in harbours,
Shaggy men in rubber boots magnificent with oars,
Cleanshaven men drying yards of netting,
Several burnt by the wind, mostly fishermen.
We specialise in the smell of seawood;
In the introvert seabirds absorbed in marine vegetation;
In high stepping waders patrolling the estuary,
Endlessly assaulting pallid molluscs.

And again the same rather unexpected imagery appears in a poem: 'The Tanker and her Tugs (Death Scene observed)' where, after describing a huge tanker entering the Carrick Roads on the full tide 'in a convoy of gulls shouting at the sun' the poet goes on to ruminate:

> What tossings in broken water before this final harbour?
> What stillnesses and becalmings?
> What revellings in foreign ports?
> What woundings, healings, contritions?
> What bouts of terrible chastity, alone with migrating birds in deserts of water?
> What undeclared cargoes?
> What inexplicable choices, with the compass faintly shaking?
> What ships passed in the night and out of the night—what ships?
> And what of those other encounters
> With the luminescent organisms that changed your course
> Off the Tierra del Fuego and the straits of Juan de Fuca,
> With the starfish clinging to the hull
> And the diabolical fish rumbling and belching
> In the catastrophic sediments?
>
> And now the sun tangles out of your rigging;
> And now Three Tugs hasten to offer
> What last assistance they may;
> Squat vessels—businesslike and composed,
> They hurry to you without fussing,
> Communicating in low voices:
> The wife? The doctor? The nurse?
> The priest with anointing oils?
>
> (The little sailing boats have caught their breath.
> Oh the efficiency in these scenes of death!)

Each in their own way, among these visiting poets I have quoted, has been equally provoked by Cornwall and its landscape (which obviously includes seascape) into a real passion of poetry. This is proof, if proof is still needed, of the validity of the theme of this book. Poets are ultra-sensitive souls and so it is hardly surprising that in their work we find such a vivid reaction. What is perhaps surprising, and certainly exciting, is the way in which a geographical background, an apparently dead land-mass, can not only stimulate such creativity—but in the process itself be somehow transformed from deadness to life. Often this creative influence inspires touches of poetic magic from quite ordinary, non-poetic writers

So we may believe
That on some day when white and piercing rays
Fuse with a water, jade and burning blue,
And foam beats on the milky shore in ecstasy,
A mortal diving deep and faithfully
Shall never die
But live forever
Knowing all
And part of thee
O glorious god, creator and destroyer
Mighty sea.
Or on a night
When white and honeyed moon
Piercing thy deepest hollow,
Leans down and calls
The black and purple waves, to rise in sapphire train
To dance and follow;
Then taking wings, like gray gulls from the granite
So every human sea-enchanted spirit
Flies out forever free in darkest space
Then sinks his rapt and star-transfigured face
To final rest in thee.

Those lines, from a poem 'Sea Magic,' are by Dora Russell, ex-wife of the late Bertrand Russell, written from her home, Carn Voel at Porthcurno. Although a prolific writer of articles Mrs Russell would probably not claim to be a poet—yet living as she does surrounded by the majestic cliffs of Treen and St Levan, aware constantly of the seething Atlantic waves rolling relentlessly over the long white sands below the Minack, she is literally *forced* into some kind of lyrical expression of her reactions.

When we come to look at the work of Cornish-born poets—and today there are a surprising number of extremely talented Cornish poets, some of them internationally known—we may often find an extra dimension in their imagery. Especially, I think, in the work of that extraordinary man, Jack Clemo, now in his fifties, who has spent his whole life in a small cottage at St Stephen, among the china-clay pits. As is possibly well known now, Jack Clemo has suffered most of his life from both blindness and deafness, but—as often fortunately happens—he has reacted to these burdens as to a challenge, and surmounted them magnificently to become one of the major poets of our time. And, of course, essentially a poet of Cornwall. . . . Fortunately in this instance the poet himself has put on record, in an article 'My Life in the Clay World', published in the CORNISH REVIEW, a penetrating assessment of the effect of Cornwall on his work as a creative artist

I was well on in my teens before I realised that there was anything symbolic about the scarred and eerie landscape which had resulted from William Cookworthy's love of pottery two hundred years earlier. I had never regarded mid-Cornwall's clay seam from a mundane standpoint, as a mere industrial product, but had simply let its elemental fantasy impress my mind and imagination. All its strong and lonely idiom was in keeping with my spiritual needs, even in childhood. Year after year I watched the clay-land dawns and sunsets, the first golden rays of the sun striking the white peaks, setting the metal prongs and tip-wires glowing and shimmering while the gravel bulk remained in shadow, and then at evening the daylight fading mysteriously from the blurred grey masses and the weird spiked clusters of stacks. At night there was a fairyland touch with the dune-lights, pit-lights and tank-lights twinkling, and the red glare of a furnace occasionally glimpsed through a kiln doorway. So many different features were revealed, some magical, some terrifying, and always free from the over-simplification sentimentality of the conventional poet's world. As I gradually became aware of the deep metaphysical undertones of this medley of restless contours—the suggestion of a purifying process leading to the "patterned cup"—I found of other parts Cornwall strangely remote from me as a poet. I saw most of Cornwall's beauty spots before I wrote any mature poems, but even St Michael's Mount did not inspire my muse, and it is only during the past two years that I have been able to reflect the rugged splendour of West Cornwall in my verse. The long obsession with clay images, and the attempt to break their grip when romance made me conscious of fertility, is the central tension of my artistic struggle.

Jack Clemo's poems speak mostly of a particular and indeed very strange part of Cornwall, the world of the silent, rearing white clay-heaps that surround his home; but with the art of a truly great poet he has managed to fuse local imagery into philosophic comment:

My Destiny is drawn
Sharp as the prongs
Of a clay-tip against the dawn,
Unsoftened by the lark's song.

Two gleaming fingers on the white snout,
Grotesque above the clotted cone
Of carnal doubt;
They are Dogma's radiant bone.

Continually Clemo uses clay-pit associations:

Sour clay faces slunk from the dream;
Ascetic contours rasped through summer haze
Beyond the lithe corn and the poppies' blaze.
Where the unmined valley
Closed in on a nudging stream,
A few stacks loomed tall and obstinate
Beside the hidden furnace, near a field gate.

And in another poem 'Clay Dams', Clemo uses the local habit of clay-damming as a physical image to portray his own religious beliefs:

> Still defiant, still immune,
> My wall of faith surrounds the soft heavings,
> Thus dammed and controlled, awaiting a heat
> Subtler than sun or switched current. No bowed bed,
> Or burst joint mars my anomalous structure,
> For it admits no fad-faked chemicals,
> That swell the flesh against traditions bounds.

Jack Clemo's poetry is earthy and harsh, even bleak—and very much the work of a Cornishman. The Cornish are, inevitably, less romantic about their county than newcomers. Much that newcomers have to learn—sometimes in painful flashes, as in John Heath-Stubb's 'This is a hideous and wicked Cornwall' is known, *instinctively*, by the Cornish-born poet. This is certainly true of Clemo, and of several other of the more articulate younger Cornish poets, like, for instance, D.M. Thomas:

> Kerenza is my name. If you betray me,
> expect no pity when the midnight moon steps forth
> and you behold me, or my enantiomorph,
> waiting for you and singing on the shore,
> My eyes, whites black as chert, will lure
> as a ship is tide-drawn to an old wharf
>
> at the tin-stream's outlet. From Bude to Geevor,
> whatever land-child you are lying with,
> you will hear a sea-child call you. Faithless wrecker,
> you will stumble down the seaward-sloping path,
> and there, by tide and rock cut off,
> trample through the red sea-running mirror,
>
> to find all changed. The lights of Perranporth
> shining as from the left side of the bay;
> kissed, it will be as if you gave
> the kiss; a black moon in an orange sky;
> a sigh beginning as a laugh
> will answer your shriek with, GIVE ME BACK THE DEAD.
>
> Then I will cling to you, your negative,
> heart clamped direct to your heart, tears
> drilling fires through your breast. Lightning from Ligger
> Head will strike the engine-house above
> you, and I will whirl you clear
> from the rocks to the running storm. For my name is Love.

In this as in much of his other work—which has been published in the U.S.A. as well as here—Thomas captures something of the sea-woven flavour running through most true Cornish imagery. He reacts equally emotionally to inland Cornwall, to places like his native Carn Brea, at Redruth, or to the moors and their ancient stones. 'These holed stones throb as I stride through stones and grass. Rain spits in my face'—in a few deft touches something mysterious is suggested. But it is to the sea-washed coast that Thomas, like so many other poets, Cornish and foreign, is drawn as if by a magnet.

> Needles flake off into the blue air. Listen.
> In the August silence, on the bare cliff path you can
> fling a stone and it will not break the silence, but
> you can hear the wedges and drills of erosion hammering
> in a silence that is uproar, beneath the wrecking
> Brissons.

That reference to mining shows a Cornishman's awareness. Awareness of a different sort is to be found in the poetry of A.L.Rowse, the *doyen* of Cornish poets. Although best known for his historical studies of the Elizabethan age—not forgetting a memorable autobiography, *A Cornish Childhood*—Rowse has continued to write delicate and nostalgic poetry that often recaptures the characteristic beauty of Cornwall's byways. He brings to life, reflectively, the quiet corners of Cornwall—the lanes around Gorran School, the little river at Hemmick winding down to a secret beach he remembers.

Another internationally known poet from Cornwall, Charles Causley, is perhaps less dependent on his native county than many of the others, in that he has achieved his success by a series of books of lyrical poems, racy and attractive, which strike home immediately to the reader anywhere. Many of these poems, like 'Farewell Aggie Weston,' commemorate a six-year period in the Royal Navy when Causley was travelling abroad. Yet when he wants to he has a capacity for illuminating our feelings about Cornwall just as effectively as the others—most notably, of course, in 'A short Life of Nevill Northey Burnard' (the Cornish sculptor). It is enough simply to quote the opening verses:

> Here lived Burnard who with his finger's bone
> Broke syllables of light from the moorstone,
> Spat on the genesis of dust and clay,
> Rubbed with huge hands the blinded eyes of day,
> And through the seasons of the talking sun
> Walked, calm as God, the fields of Altarnum.

Here, where St Nonna with a holy reed
Hit the bare granite, made the waters bleed,
Madmen swam to their wits in her tin well,
Young Burnard fasted, watched, learned how to tell
Stone beads under the stream, and at its knock
Quietly lifted out his prize of rock.

There are older Cornish-born poets of eminence, men like the playwright Ronald Duncan at Morwenstow, engaged on writing an epic poem on 'Man', many thousands of lines long; or like Ronald Bottrall, from Camborne, who was published internationally at the time of Auden and Spender and Isherwood. And even those originally of Cornish stock who have travelled literally to the ends of the earth, like Allen Curnow, now a professor at Auckland University, New Zealand, can never really forget.

Curnow of Anlebra farm at Nancledra, Curnow the sweep,
Curnow of the mercer and councillor, Curnow the barber,
Curnow of Gurnard's Head over by Wikka where deep
In the scoop of the Western swell your grey hulk's harbour

Death, fisher of man, your nets of granite and foam;
Surely you haul us all in, the shoal of our lives,
Mine of a strange sea native, Pacific my home,
And my tribes folk, men of your tetrarchate, Saint Ives.

I hear in a winter mist the drowned moan over the moors
And the Zennor Maid sing scorn on the Body and Blood
Green-lashing the moon in her hair and the souls of her wooers,
The beast-girl's image graven in the house of God:

Lithe-tailed Lilith we loved in our sea dreams;
The cross in her sea-glass dangles upside down,
Down, down, deep as the locked Antartic streams
And the blind isles where the bread of my birth was thrown—

Void as all voyages, for the mast of her mirror
Chases and faces: all constellations glitter
On the surf of her song, the tide's tongue of her terror
Since the gadfly God-word skimmed her curdlipped water.

In Allen Curnow's poem is to be found in abundance all that strange and particularised imagery which seems to be drawn out of poets when they come into contact with Cornwall. Whether Tennyson or Hardy, Graham or Heath-Stubbs, Clemo or Thomas or Curnow—the accident of being born in Cornwall is seen to be not so important. What *is* important—significant and inexplicable—is the effect of the land (and sea) upon the human creative worker, in this case the poets. Jack Clemo spelled things out for us when he reflected upon his life in the clay world, and talked of 'the deep metaphysical undertones of this medley of restless contours'. Clemo was referring to the world of the clay-pits that surrounds him, but in Cornwall there are many worlds to surround the creators, and it would be surprising if they did not respond with passion and power—mixed, as ever in Cornwall, with a little sadness.

I see in dreams the lost land of Langarrow
Sleeping under silent sandy waves;
In every house and every roadway narrow
The dry bones stir in their unquiet graves.
On sand-soft pillows in a dry, cold kiss
Skull touches skull as even on that night
They lay without a thought of aught amiss
Until the drifting sand blocked out their light.
The yellowing bones within the taverns cry
For wine to clear their parching throat of sand;
And now those bones forever are as dry
As those dice they rattled in their hand.
Seven churches stood within the walls,
Far-famed their slender towers and stately piers,
Their priests grew fat within the prince's halls,
Their bells are silent now these many years.
The merchants' business now no longer thrives,
The golden sand invades their golden hoards
And chokes the mouths that chaffered for men's lives
And bartered bodies over counter boards.
The dry bones' rustle fills the sand-sunk town,
Whispering the tales of shame and lust
That brought a rich and powerful kingdom down
And closed its people's eyes with yellow dust.

I cannot do better than close this chapter with that lament by Richard G. Jenkin, a Cornish Bard. Like the painters, the poets give us the colour and the imagery—the rest is up to us. We would surely be very lacking in imaginative response if, reading some of the poetry I have been quoting, we did not encounter an impression that perhaps, indeed, we are dealing with worlds, a place—a county, if we must use such a mundane word—very different from most others.

V

Du Maurier Land

PERHAPS it is no accident that some of the world's most popular novelists have set their books in Cornwall. Daphne du Maurier, Howard Spring, Winston Graham—to quote but three names—have all made international reputations with work that is steeped in the mystery and strangeness of the county in which they all made their homes. Nor perhaps is it entirely accidental that none of these writers is Cornish-born: that is, they have been drawn to Cornwall from more conventional zones, lured by that very romantic atmosphere which in turn they have captured in their novels.

Is this really so very surprising? Who, for instance, driving over Bodmin Moor and suddenly coming upon the forlorn outline of the now famous Jamaica Inn, at Bolventor, can fail to feel the impact of such a stark, bleak out-of-this-world setting? How well, in turn, did Daphne du Maurier capitalize upon this atmosphere in her best-seller, *Jamaica Inn*, deepening the shadows, stressing the unease, heightening the general impression of eeriness, of other-worldliness. Consider, for instance, this portrayal of the landlord, Joss:

> He was a great husk of a man, nearly seven feet high, with a creased black brow and the skin the colour of a gypsy. His thick dark hair fell over his eyes in a fringe and hung about his ears. He looked as if he had the strength of a horse with immense powerful shoulders, long arms that reached almost to his knees, and large fists like hams. His frame was so big that in a sense his head was dwarfed, and sunk between his shoulders, giving that half stooping impression of a giant gorilla, with his black eyebrows and his mat of hair. But for all his long limbs and mighty frame, there was nothing of the ape about his features for his nose was hooked, curving to a mouth that might have been perfect once but now sunken and fallen, and there was still something fine about his great dark eyes, in spite of the lines and pouches and the red blood flecks.

This is writing larger than life—and therefore eminently suited to a Cornish novel. Miss Du Maurier herself has in other tales used equally vivid descriptive passages to portray the place as well as people—in *Rebecca*, *Frenchman's Creek*, *My Cousin Rachel*, there are haunting descriptions of wild cliffs, raging seas, bleak, lonely spots of a kind that it often seems are only found in Cornwall. In one of her most recent novels, *The House on the Strand*, Miss Du Maurier took that familiar Cornish legend of land that had disappeared under the sea and gave it an unfamiliar modern twist by portraying a man who, under the influence of a potent drug, was able to return to the time when that land was still above the sea.

In a way, here is a perfect example of Cornwall stirring the creative faculties. It is of course perfectly possible to make a case for suggesting that Daphne du Maurier *might* have written all her novels, attained the same popularity, if she had spent her whole life living in Tooting or Surbiton. No doubt a writer of such talent would have dug some kind of romance and mystery even out of such mundane settings. But it is still difficult to imagine that she would have produced *quite* such haunting, disturbing, other-worldly atmospheres. Without entering into too many arguments on the point, one is entitled to declare that Tooting is *not* Cornwall—that there *is* some kind of elemental difference between a suburban London street and the cliffs of Land's End; between the glittering West End shops and the equally glittering but much older Dozmary Pool or Looe Bar; between the unseen yet unforgettable Land of Lyonesse, and the very much seen and (a lot of people might feel) utterly forgettable building-estates of the North Circular Road.

Another novelist who had good reason to recognise this difference (having grown up in the slums of Cardiff and later lived in the heart of smoky Manchester) was Howard Spring. His novels are much more literal and less dependant on ghostliness and haunting than those of Miss Du Maurier, yet in their own way they have done just as much to awaken the world's curiosity about Cornwall. Here is Spring's first impression of Falmouth Harbour, the area where he was to spend the last three decades of his life:

The sea sweeps into a magnificent harbour, and off the harbour run broad arms of water—now blue, now green—that feel their way deep into the recesses of the hills; and themselves in many cases throw off other arms that go in countless ramifications through the countryside. All are subject to the sea, so that the surge and sigh of waters governed by the steadfast laws of the tides draw music through all the hollows of the hills. Great ships go up and anchor deep in the heart of the country; and at every turning one may come upon an inland village with a sweep of shingle beach, a tiny jetty, and a marine flavour.

No motor-car or char-a-banc disturbed the quiet; to get from place to place, if one did not want to walk twenty miles, one used a boat to cross the blue shining fiords. At twilight doors one came suddenly on old twilight men, telescope to eye, following the fortunes of vessels they had known more intimately. In sunny gardens palms grew to a splendid height, and the intense colours of the sea, seen between their stems, gave to the landscape a sub-tropical illusion. Then there was the blue and green transparent water of the sea and the creeks inviting the body to its cold embrace; and there were farms where old memories might be revived of 'three-decker' teas—splits and butter, jam and cream piled on top of one another. Not least of the charms was the name of one particular stretch of the country—Roseland.

Howard Spring was an extremely professional writer, with years of journalistic training, and so in his novels one finds a great deal of exact reportage, with the most detailed and accurate scene-painting, as in this passage from his last novel, *Winds of the Day*:

I stood there alone. Dros-y-Mor has now become an accustomed house to me, but I wish to write of what I saw then. I stood with my back to it and looked upon the creek. This twisted a hundred yards or so from the house, so that I saw little of it. But I saw and felt the quietness: the fields that sloped down to the water, the heron wading along the shore, a tree here and there mirrored in the glass of the water, a swan making for the bank with a flotilla of brown cygnets behind it. The water ended at my feet, arrested by a wall that had been built up of the local stone, and to my right stone steps climbed to this grassy platform on which I stood. It had that day been shorn, and the smell of cut grass was all about me, filling the air which trembled now on the verge of night, with the new moon going down. I turned and looked at the house that had been behind me, long and low and white. The tall trees, bursting into full leaf, rose behind it, sheltering it with great arms, birch and elm and sycamore. The stream that ran through them here met the sea. A ghostly tinkle of water, as it tumbled over one edge of the platform, was in my ears, and there, glimmering now, their gold turning dark, the king-cups grew.

In Spring's most famous novel, *My Son, My Son*, the hero and narrator goes to join a friend staying in Falmouth:

It was the first time I had travelled into the West Country, and once I had crossed the Saltash Bridge, leaving Devonshire behind, and had entered upon the strange, riven countryside of Cornwall, with the railway passing over viaduct after viaduct, carrying us above chasms filled with dusky woods, and through tilted, angular pastures, and alongside the great white cones of the clay works that rose against the sky like giants' tents, and giving us here and there glimpses of a distant sea bluer than any I had known, and nearer views of unaccustomed vegetation, eucalyptus and palm and a profusion of hydrangeas; why, then I felt the North fall like a smoky burden from my back and a deep willingness for lotus-eating take possession of me.

Spring, in this quieter, more even approach, still eventually conveys much the same message as Daphne du Maurier—in almost every one of his novels that have a Cornish setting (and few have not, in the later years) he is constantly stressing that magical moment when one 'enters upon the strange riven countryside of Cornwall'—or when 'I felt the

North fall like a smoky burden from my back'—in other words, he recognises that Cornwall is not as other places, but a world apart.

As an earlier, even greater novelist put it succinctly in a letter, 'We go to Cornwall on Thursday. That is the beginning.'

For D. H. Lawrence, who in 1916–17 lived at Higher Tregerthen, Zennor, Cornwall was to be merely a passing phase. Yet a writer of his genius would have been incapable of not reacting to such a sensitized place. In his letters he wrote enthusiastically of the magnificent scenery, the seas breaking against the rocks 'like the first craggy breaking of dawn in the world'—a great comfort after all 'this whirlwind of dust and grit and dirty paper of a modern Europe.'

> I do like Cornwall. It is still something like King Arthur and Tristan. It has never taken the Anglo-Saxon civilisation, the Anglo-Saxon sort of Christianity. One can feel free here for that reason—feel the world as it was in that flicker of pre-Christian civilisation when humanity was really young.

Paradoxically (like the poet Heath-Stubbs, who also spent periods in Zennor) Lawrence did not take to the Cornish people, though acknowledging in them a natural gentleness.

> I don't like the people here. They ought to be living in the darkness and warmth and passionateness of the blood, sudden, incalculable. Whereas they are like insects gone cold, living only for money, *for dirt* . . . . They are all afraid—that's why they are so mean. But I don't really understand them. Only I know this, I have never in my life come across such inertly selfish people.

Lawrence of course, was given to somewhat exaggerated off-the-cuff intuitions—yet he *was* a genius, and there *is* perception in his criticism, as well as his praise—'The Cornish have had a harsh, unprotected life and in order to survive they have had to withdraw into their shells —this often seeming, to an outsider, self-centred, or selfish.'

Later on, Lawrence proposed to Middleton Murray and Katherine Mansfield that they and other writers should

> live here, pitch our camp and unite our forces and become an active power, here, together . . . It is a most beautiful place, a tiny village nestling under high, shaggy moorhills, a big sweep of lovely sea beyond, such lovely sea, lovelier than the Mediterranean. It is five miles from St Ives and seven miles from Penzance. To Penzance one goes over the moors, high, then down into Mount's Bay, all gorse now, flickering with flowers; and then it will be heather; and then hundreds of foxgloves. It's the best place I have been in.

In the years ahead there were other places to draw Lawrence—France, Italy, Mexico. But probably only in the last-named did he feel quite as close to the elemental as he did in West Cornwall in that 'splendid place' on the edge of a few rough stony fields that go to the sea, where 'there is a little grassy terrace outside and at the back the moor tumbles down, great enormous grey boulders and gorse. . . . It would be so *splendid* if it could come off; such a lovely place; our Rananim.'

Lawrence was never to find his Rananim, but his instincts were on the right lines. Before and since, many other artists have been equally tempted by the dramatic background of Cornwall to make it a centre for group-living. In a sense, this is what the artists have done, turning whole areas like St Ives and Newlyn into their own community centres. Writers being much more individualistic, real loners, perhaps one cannot expect quite the same achievement. Yet it is surely significant how many writers have been drawn to Cornwall, even if only briefly like Lawrence.

Virginia Woolf, whose literary eminence was achieved at much the same time as Lawrence, was a totally different kind of writer, though in her own way just as much a genius. Yet, she too, was inexplicably affected by Cornwall, and in particular the same corner as Lawrence knew —the area around St Ives Bay stretching from Godrevy in the East to Zennor and Gurnard's Head in the West. Unlike Lawrence, Virginia Woolf spent many long periods in Cornwall, where her father, the critic Leslie Stephen, had a house in St Ives. From the window of this house young Virginia could look out on a panoramic view of the vast sweep of St Ives Bay in which, pre-eminent, stands out the white lighthouse of Godrevy. Many years later that setting, that lighthouse indeed, was to provide the background for one of Virginia Woolf's most famous novels, *To the Lighthouse*. It is very much an intellectual's book, and yet constantly in the descriptive passages, even if put into people's mouths as conversational pieces, the images and influences of Cornwall are forever breaking through. Like every other major writer who has ever visited Cornwall, Virginia Woolf never forgot the extraordinary impact of that wild, elemental, indeed quite fantastic land.

Another internationally famous novelist to base many of his tales on Cornwall, where he spent a decade living at Perranporth, is Winston Graham. Like Daphne du Maurier, Graham has been drawn irresistibly to the past—not surprisingly, for the past of Cornwall is rich in sources of inspiration for serious writers of fiction; religion, piracy, wrecking, mining, the land, are all themes with a large appeal. Winston Graham is one of those rare writers who manages to create imaginatively from factual evidence. He is a great believer in using only known facts, and endless research went into his most famous series, the Poldark Books—*Ross Poldark*, *Demelza*, *Jeremy Poldark* and *Warleggan*. This is really one continuous novel, covering in minute detail the period 1783–1793, a time of rapid transformation in the economic and spiritual life of a county, where the currents of rural and seafaring activities intermingled and were also affected by mining and its affiliated interests. In case this sounds dull stuff let me hasten to say it is quite the reverse. Here is what that perceptive literary critic, Ernest Martin, had to say:

> The value of a work of this length and range lies in its imagination and its care for detail. All long chronicles of family life tend to lose their impetus at some points. Mr Graham has created characters who live on in the mind. Ross and Demelza and Dr Enys, Caroline Penvenen and the Warleggans are all convincing persons with their own identities, and the long account of their lives does not flag. In common with other counties, Cornwall shares in an existence subjected to the demands of tourism on the one hand and the threat of environmental devastation on the other. Therefore it is not just escapism to project the mind back in time and live again in the calm of the old Cornwall. It must also be a kind of fulfilment.

Du Maurier, Howard Spring, D. H. Lawrence, Virginia Woolf, Winston Graham, Compton Mackenzie, J. D. Beresford, Thomas Hardy, Margaret Kennedy, Guy Thorne—more recently, Leo Walmsley, Walter Greenwood, Ronald Fraser, Frank Baker, Colin Wilson, Ronald Duncan—the list of authors of novels about or inspired by Cornwall, can be an endless one. Further back still there are R. M. Ballantyne, best known as the author of *Coral Island*, who wrote an early novel, *Deep Down, a Tale of the Cornish Mines*, following a period living in Penzance; 'Q' (Sir Arthur Quiller-Couch), who immortalised the little port of Fowey in a series of Toy Town novels; and the famous parson, S. Baring-Gould, whose work is even now regularly reprinted and selling in huge quantities.

Sometimes the Cornish influences come as a surprise. How many people, for instance, realise that Cornwall was very much involved in the creation of *The Wind in the Willows*? Kenneth Graham, author of that classic, visited Cornwall constantly, spending holidays at the Lizard, St Ives, Falmouth and, in particular, Fowey, his favourite spot. In the chapter entitled 'Wayfarers All' there is this picture of a typical Cornish sea-port of the nineteenth century, in the words of the Sea Rat:

> 'And now,' he was softly saying, 'I take to the road again, holding on southwestwards for many a long and dusty day: till at last I reach the little grey sea town I know so well, that clings along one steep side of the harbour. There through dark doorways you look down flights of stone steps, overhung by great pink tufts of valerian and ending in a patch of sparkling blue water. The little boats that lie tethered to the rings and stanchions of the old see-wall are gaily

painted as those I clambered in an out of in my own childhood: the salmon leap on the flood tide, schools of mackerel flash and play past quay-sides and foreshores, and by the windows the great vessels glide, night and day, up to their moorings or forth to the open sea. There, sooner or later, the ships of all seafaring nations arrive; and there, at its destined hour the ship of my choice will let go its anchor. I shall take my time, I shall tarry and bide, till at last the right one lies waiting for me, warped out into midstream, loaded low, her bow-sprit pointing down harbour. I shall slip on board, by boat or along hauser; and then one morning I shall wake to the song and tramp of the sailors, the clink of the capstan, and the rattle of the anchor-chain coming merrily in. We shall break out the jib and the foresail, the white houses on the harbour side will glide slowly past us as she gathers steeringway, and the voyage will have begun! As she forges towards the headland she will clothe herself with canvas; and then, once outside, the sounding slap of great green seas as she heels to the wind, pointing south!'

There are many other glimpses of Cornwall woven into the fabric of *The Wind in the Willows* (not least in importance being what appears to be a description of the recent home of the author of this book, The Old Sawmills at Golant, above Fowey):

Leaving the main stream, they now passed into what seemed at first sight like a little land-locked lake. Green turf sloped down to either edge, brown snaky tree roots gleamed below the surface of the quiet water, while ahead of them the silvery shoulder and foamy tumble of a weir, arm in arm with a restless dripping mill wheel, that held up in its turn a grey-gabled mill house, filled the air with a soothing murmur of sound, dull and smothering yet with little clear voices speaking up cheerfully out of it at intervals. It was so very beautiful that the Mole could only hold up both fore paws and gasp, 'O my! O my! O my!'

This, of course, is the quieter, more peaceful side of Cornwall—which does indeed exist up rivers like the Fal and Fowey. Somehow, though, it is not these areas in general that have inspired either writers or painters. Novelists have instinctively been drawn by the more mysterious side of Cornwall, those facets which are at once subterranean and yet, in a way, all-pervading. How fortunate, for instance, has been the novelist Ruth Manning-Sanders to spend a large part of her working-life living high up on the cliffs at Sennen Cove. Small wonder that—recollecting a walk out on to Land's End in the twilight of a wintry afternoon, when nothing was to be seen but the huge dim shapes of the silently withdrawn cliffs and the red rhythmically winking eye of the Longships lighthouse—she wrote:

It is then that the drowned sailors of the past can be heard hailing their names above the moaning of the waters. It is then that the sense of the primordial, the strange and the savage, the unknown, the very long ago, fills the dusk with something that is akin to dread. It is then that the place becomes haunted; a giant heaves grey limbs from his granite bed; a witch sits in that stone chair on the cliff . . .

In a way it may seem surprising there have not been more ghost novels about Cornwall . . . In fact down the centuries there have accumulated a vast collection of basic Cornish ghost stories (many of them collected in a series by Mrs Manning-Sanders). What contemporary novelists have done is not so much repeat familiar old mysteries, as to use the same ghostly background, the haunted Cornwall touch, in which to elaborate their more personal themes. It is not difficult to find such backgrounds—even evil ones. Cornwall has evil as well as good buried in its great granite boulders—a factor well understood by 'The Beast', Aleister Crowley, who lived for some time at Newlyn, outside Penzance, and is supposed to have conducted many Black Masses in the area.

Black Masses would not somehow seem surprising in Cornwall—just as almost any other eccentricity seems more acceptable in the Cornish setting. It is no accident that Cornwall is an obvious haven for the beatnik, the drop-outs, the beautiful people. In Cornwall there is always an underlying sense that anything and perhaps everything can and does happen.

To live in such a place, to be made aware physically of the vast and imponderable nature of the universe, may be disturbing but, for a novelist at least, it is stimulating, a challenge. Many a young novelist who has later gone farther out into the world, has spent his almost obligatory year or two living in some lonely Cornish cottage. I did myself, once inhabiting a castle at Portquin, later a cowshed on Trencom, still later Bernard Walke's old vicarage at St Hilary. In each of these places I received impressions and influences whose impact I shall never forget. In particular, I remember walking on the magical face of Trencom by moonlight, when the giants were surely stirring in their uneasy sleep—looking from the winking light of Godrevy on one side to the twinkling night-city of Penzance in the South—and feeling a strange sense of being part of a world quite beyond the understanding of London, Birmingham or Manchester.

This sense, I think, is conveyed quite often in many lesser known novels about Cornwall. You will certainly find it in the work of Frank Baker, widely known for his best-seller *Miss Hargreaves*, but author also of several Cornish novels like *Embers* and *The Downs so Free.* In an article in an early issue of the CORNISH REVIEW Frank Baker wrote perceptively of the effect of Cornwall upon a young writer living in a lonely cottage by Cape Cornwall, in Kenidzhak Valley:

At last I came to the gate and swung it aside. Down came the smell of stock, sensuously opening out to me in the spring flowering of the hillside. The warm moisture of the flower-filled night surged into me and drew me also deep into its living centre. I was an operative part now of all this, I said, as I climbed the last bit of steep path past the almost invisible beds of bulb flowers. I paused by the well, listening to the blackbird singing wildly from the stone hedge at the bottom, an outpouring of ecstatic song which touched the strings of my heart and called out to music there. The wind blew from the west, and it was warm. Into my head came a melody for the four-line Elizabethan lyric I had always wanted to set;

> O Western wind, when wilt thou blow
> That the small rain down can rain?
> Christ, that my love were in my arms,
> And I in my bed again!

Yes, I would compose, I told myself. Later, I would find a cottage, get a piano down, set those lines, and Flecker's *Don Juan*; score for string quartet and oboe the setting of Keat's *Ode to Autumn* which I knew I had it inside me to write. Or should it be the first novel? For this was simmering to come to flame in me. The novel (like all first novels) which should tell an unlistening world all that I had to tell it about Frank Baker and his world. Novel, or song? I was not sure. The usual sweat of indecision was upon me. Caught in excitement between the two choices—music or writing—I went past the well with its trailing periwinkle to the stone steps outside the only door to *Edge o' Beyond.* First slight anxiety. Would the key be where Maxie had said it was—under a particular stone? I felt; and after a little fumbling, found it. Next slight anxiety. Would I be able to open the door? It had always been tricky, so seldom was it locked; we had had trouble with it on our return from these long summer walks, I remembered. I tried it. After a turn or two, the lock yielded. The door of my newly found freedom opened to me.

Of course it would be possible to go on quoting endlessly from the words of novelists themselves in order to show the extreme relevance of Cornwall on their work. What is perhaps most interesting is the variety of that influence. Most novelists, naturally—like the poets and the painters—are irresistibly drawn by the sheer majesty and picturesqueness of the Cornish background. But then there is another side to the coin altogether, the simplicity offered to the creative worker by life far far away from that maddening crowd (yes, even with today's holiday invasions, which after all only last for a brief spell). Few novelists have expressed this side of the coin better than the late Leo Walmsley, who for many years lived in a tiny bungalow on the side of Pont Creek, by Polruan and opposite Fowey. For many of the personal details I would recommend readers to delve into Walmsley's autobiographical books *Paradise Creek* and *Angler's Moon.* But it was in a novel, *Love in the Sun*, that Walmsley created a portrayal of the simple life in Cornwall that was to be a literary best-seller. This simple story of a man and a girl coming to Fowey and finding a hut on the shores of a creek, renting it for a few bob a week, making their own furniture, growing vegetables, fishing for food, having a baby, being poor but very happy, seems to appeal strongly to people in this rat-race age.

Cornwall, of course, is not the only place where you can get away from it all: that, from the point of view of this particular book, is not the primary point. What interests me about Cornwall is what it is that the writer—the artist, the poet, the potter—gets away *to*. For there is something there that is very unusual, very much subterranean, and very, very potent. As the novelist Thomas Burke once commented: ' . . . there is little one can say . . . Description conveys nothing, and reflections are meaningless. What it has to give must be received individually . . . . '

Even Britain's greatest novelist, Charles Dickens, came under the spell, and probably appreciated Thomas Burke's remark only too well. When he was only 30, Dickens made a walking tour of the Duchy in the company of the literary critic, John Forster. Immediately the great man's imagination was fired, and enthusiastically he told Forster that he would open his next novel 'in some terribly iron-bound spot' on the Cornish Coast . . .

Such a trip as we had into Cornwall, just after Longfellow went away. We sent down to Devonshire by rail-road and there we hired an open carriage from an inn keeper patriotic in these Pickwick matters, and went on with post-horses. Sometimes we travelled all night, sometimes all day, sometimes both. I kept the joint stock purse, ordered all the dinners, paid the turnpikes, conducted facetious conversations with post-boys and regulated the pace at which we travelled.

If you could have followed us into the earthy old churches and into the strange caverns of the gloomy seashore, and down into the depths of mines, and up to the top of giddy heights where unspeakable green water was roaring. If you could have seen but one gleam of the bright fires by which we sat in the big rooms of ancient inns at night, until long after the small hours had come and gone, or smelt but one steam of the hot punch which came in every evening in a huge broad china bowl. I never laughed so much in my life as I did on this journey.

Many years later Dickens returned, this time with his friend Wilkie Collins, author of *The Woman in White* and other macabre stories. Not surprisingly, Collins was especially receptive to the strange atmosphere of Cornwall, about which he wrote a whole chapter in a book *Rambles beyond Railways*. He went down the Botallack Mine and also investigated the life of the fishermen: with his novelist's eye for the out-of-the-way he uncovered many strange stories, like this he found in Mawgan churchyard, near Newquay:

Within the churchyard the bright colour of the turf, and grey hues of the mouldering tombstones, are picturesquely intermingled all over the uneven surface of the ground, save in one remote corner, where the graves are few and the grass grows rank and high. Here the eye is abruptly attracted to the stern of a boat, painted white, and fixed upright in the earth. This strange memorial, little suited though it be to the old monuments around, has a significance of its own which gives it a peculiar claim to consideration. Inscribed on it appeared the names of ten fishermen of the parish who went out to sea to pursue their calling, on one wintry night in 1846. It was unusually cold on land—on the sea the frosty, bitter wind cut through the bones. The men were badly provided against the weather; and, hardy as they were, the weather killed them that night. In the morning the boat drifted on shore, manned like a spectre bark by the ghastly figures of the dead—freighted horribly with the corpses of ten men all frozen to death. They are now buried in Mawgan Churchyard, and the stern of the boat they died in tells their fatal story, and points to the last home which they share together.

This incident is all part of the eerie mosaic that makes up the Cornish pattern. So much of what happens in Cornwall is larger than life. Wrecks, storms, gales, mine disasters, clay mountains and haunted moors—nothing is quite normal: And this is responded to, instinctively, by writers and painters—in particular, as one might expect, by the novelists, with their eye for the sheer drama of it all.

Paradoxically, at least among novelists, few Cornish-born writers seem to respond in quite the same way. It is as if, perhaps by their blood-link, they have been partially immunised. The two novelists Joseph and Silas K. Hocking are good examples, for though in their time they became famous purveyors of popular novels of the day for the masses, their Cornish origin was almost irrelevant. Jack Clemo, a distant relative, once wrote of them that despite the fact they and he were sons of the same parish, and that possibly his talent derived from them, he felt that he had lived all his life in a Cornwall they never knew, and could never have attempted to describe.

In considering them as Cornish writers, therefore, we have to notice certain inhibitions that may have resulted from the early struggle which made the associations of their childhood distasteful to them when they had escaped to a higher social level. In Silas's reminiscences, *My Book of Memory*, there are practically no Cornish scenes; he records nothing of those poverty-stricken early years in the dour little cottage on Terras Moor, the narrow flat waste between Meledor and St Stephens. The clayworks, with their powerful symbolism, the idiom of the new, industrial Cornwall, were beginning to scar the hillsides all round when Joseph and Silas left home for college. This fresh land, teeming with craggy and purgatorial images, awaited its interpreter: there was religious mystery in the crossed tip-beams pointing skyward; erotic mystery in the sharp white breasts of rock that were cleansed for the kiln-bed. But the Hockings saw these features only as signs of a messy industry with which they had no concern. They turned away to the fashionable world which provided them with material for naive tales of society life and for Silas's book of amusing anecdotes about the celebrities he had met.

To accuse them of dishonesty to the Cornwall they had known would be easy, but hardly just; for they had known it only with the surface of their minds, that surface which registered normal tastes and reactions. They were rendered impotent as creators and interpreters by the very wholesomeness of their mental texture. Silas in his later years condemned modern novelists of the D. H. Lawrence calibre as 'excessively morbid'; but the key to all original interpretation lies in the abnormality of approach that is usually called morbid. Lawrence evoked more of the essential Cornish character in a dozen pages of *Kangaroo* than the Hockings could do in a score of novels—precisely because he was 'morbid,' reacting simply and sensuously with the living flow of his subconscious mind. But the Hockings did not even attempt the superficial yet detailed portrayal of the Cornish background which we find in such novels as Crosbie Garstin's *The Owl's House* and Compton Mackenzie's *Carnival*. . . .

Jack Clemo goes on to draw the interesting conclusion that what was lacking was the true Celtic vision, the vision that should rise instinctively in an imagination which is an off shoot of centuries of semi-tribal blood intimacy under the Christian symbols:

D. H. Lawrence felt this primitiveness in the Cornish people, yet until recent years no Cornish writer had even hinted at its existence. 'Q' wrote on a far higher intellectual and artistic level than the Hockings, but he was as devoid as they of this elemental mystic awareness, the sense of 'mud and Godhead' in the Cornish texture. Did they leave the county too soon before it had really spoken to them? Or was there an innate fastidiousness that made them recoil to the protection of civilised and cultured life? They certainly lacked the Celtic capacity for obsessions *which might be expected to show itself in Cornish writers no less than Welsh and Irish ones.*

The italics are mine, for I feel that Jack Clemo has put his finger on a crucial point. Why I do not know and cannot explain, but there does appear to be this blanketting off of the natural Celtic creativeness among the Cornish. As I have shown here and there a Cornish poet of genius, like Clemo himself, breaks through the shadows. But in general such Cornish writers as there have been have remained second class. This becomes most evident if we consider the richness of Welsh literature—Dylan Thomas, Vernon Watkins, Caradoc Evans, Gwyn Jones, Glyn Jones, Gwyn Thomas, Richard Llewellyn: or Irish—Frank O'Connor, James Joyce, G. S. Shaw, 'A. E.', Yeats, Liam O'Flaherty, Sean O'Faolain, Sean O'Casey. There is just no comparison . . . and this is a great pity because in seeking to understand the mysterious qualities of Cornwall we would benefit greatly from the interpretations and articulations of truly native figures.

Instead we have to look to the eternal 'foreigner' for our evidence. Fortunately, as I hope I have been able to indicate, there are plenty of persuasive exponents. Something about Cornwall and its settings, particularly its sea-washed coastline, as I have said, seems to bring out splendour in writing. I am thinking now as I write of a novelist I have not yet mentioned, Frank Baines, who spent all his early childhood on the Lizard, and has commemorated those years most brilliantly in *Look towards the Sea.* In that book there is an unforgettable recollection of a famous Cornish event, the wreck of the s.s. *Mohecan* on the Manacles. Read it, and you capture a large slice of the truly dramatic Cornish life *which is yet almost everyday experience.* Here is how Baines concludes:

> The end of this story is pure myth. It tells of a strange man at dawn at Helford Passage. Down through Newgan and Manaccan this stranger had been traced from St Keverne during the night. Seaweed was his hair and barnacles his knuckles and his eyes were open and starey and perfectly unblinking. He seemed to have difficulty in closing the lids. He sat with a hand up to shield his face from the light. Over his arm he carried a jacket folded inside out, and had been helping with the wreck, he said. Some noticed that there was gold braid on his cuffs and shoulders, and they took him for a sailor. Tradition had it he was the captain of the *Mohecan.* Did George see him plunge into the sea? Could he have saved himself and escaped in this matter or was it a ghost?

Or was it a ghost? In Cornwall the question seems a perfectly normal one; much that is unnatural, and even supernatural, somehow becomes absorbed, and almost natural. Translate many of the great novels about Cornwall, set them in some conventional non-supernatural setting —and probably they would be read as artificial and false. They would certainly lack some kind of underlying power and strength. I do not think many novelists, alive or dead, would deny the incalculable effect that Cornwall has had upon their writing.

VI

The Stuff of Drama

IN CORNWALL the word 'drama' can be said to have a rather wider interpretation than in most other places. After all, in many ways drama—everyday drama—has been the very stuff of life in many parts of the county. Rebellions, mine disasters, shipwrecks, and other dramatic events have been commonplace in a land so exposed to the elements. As a consequence there has always been a tendency for the theatrical touch to play a prominent part in local affairs. It has, however, been very much an amateur business—the professional theatre has always failed to gain any firm footing in the county. This is sad, certainly, but it has not been a disaster. In its place there are probably more amateur dramatic societies, more brass bands, more carnivals, more Feast Days, than in most other parts of Britain. The Cornish, and the people who have gone to live in Cornwall, have made their own drama.

This all dates back to before the Reformation, when Cornish was still the language of Cornwall, and the county was the setting for a whole series of the famous Miracle Plays. For many years these plays were lost, and then in 1860 the series of Cornish plays grouped under the heading *Bewnans Meryasek*, written in 1504, were discovered in a library in Wales. From the text one realises that the plays were long-drawn-out affairs. Indeed in days when travel was a difficult business, those who went to see the plays in one of the numerous Plain an Gwarry, or 'playing places' (there is one such amphitheatre in St Just, another at Perran Round) would make a proper holiday of the outing, camping out for several days in the fields around. The plays took two or three days to perform and after each day's play there was an invitation from the stage to drinking, dancing and cockfighting, entertainment that came to be regarded as sinful after the Reformation. After falling into disrepute, the plays were revived by Cornish scholars in the middle of this century, and a performance of *Bewnans Meryasek* was put on during the Celtic Congress at Truro, in 1950. Here is an account by the producer, Helena Charles:

At first, to us, the play appeared more of an archaeological curiosity than a drama. It was left to Mrs Collingwood Selby, the County Drama Organiser, to point out to us the dramatic and comic possibilities of the play, and to help us to demonstrate these to an audience, most of whom did not understand Cornish. The measure of her success can be gauged by the remark of a small boy in St Day who saw a later performance of what he described as 'Some 'ansome play.' After 400 years part of Camborne's play was performed by Camborne-Redruth people in Truro, St Day, Redruth and Camborne.

Owing to the support of Mrs Collingwood Selby the play was included as an associate production of the Cornwall Amateur Drama Festival, the only play in Cornish to be produced during the Festival. The only Plain an Gwarry that is in good state of preservation is at St Just, and the surroundings of this are uninteresting. Of all possible sites, unquestionably the most attractive was Perran Round. The origins of this circular fortification with a diameter of 50 yards are uncertain. It is probably an Iron Age Camp. There are those who deny that it was a medieval theatre, but the traces of tiers in the bank indicate that performances of some kind took place there, and, whether it was the sixteenth or the twentieth century that discerned its virtues as a theatre is irrelevant.

The play itself was very short, deliberately, owing to the strangeness of the language. It told the story of the clash between Meryasek, who lived at Camborne, 'a little to the west of Carn Brea', and the heathen King Teudar, who tried unsuccessfully to catch and kill the Christian Saint. Meryasek, having blessed his rock, and prayed that his well may be for the healing of insanity and disease, asks a sea-captain who conveniently appears, to take him to Brittany. It has been suggested that the ditch and depression that almost divide half of Perran Round in two, may have been used in early performances of the play to separate Cornwall from Brittany. We decided on this for the final episode. Saint and sailors step across the ditch, and a sailor says:

> Tremenys yu dyogel
> Lemmyn genen au chanel
> ('Now the channel is safely crossed by us')

As the Saint leaves the stage, the seaman sees the off stage rock, bowing down to receive him, and cries out at the miracle.

We planned our programme to correspond as nearly as possible with the festivities of medieval times. After the play the M.C. called the original invitation from this play, for piping and dancing. A recorder band from Camborne County School struck up the Helston Furry, and the Portreath Folk Dance Group and dancers from St Ives led the audience in the Furry and the Helston Country Dance which, till 1914, was always danced immediately after the Furry.

Cornish and Breton dancing was followed by traditional and modern songs in Cornish, by a display of wrestling, and finally an impressive rendering in Cornish of 'Land of our Fathers' and 'Shall Trelawney Die?' sung by the Skinners Bottom Male Voice Choir, standing bare-headed and to attention, while outside the Round, St Perran's Cross, the ancient flag of Cornwall fluttered in the breeze. A B.B.C. commentator described the entertainment as 'nationalist'. Be that as it may, Anglo-Saxon it was not, and those who, from ignorance or

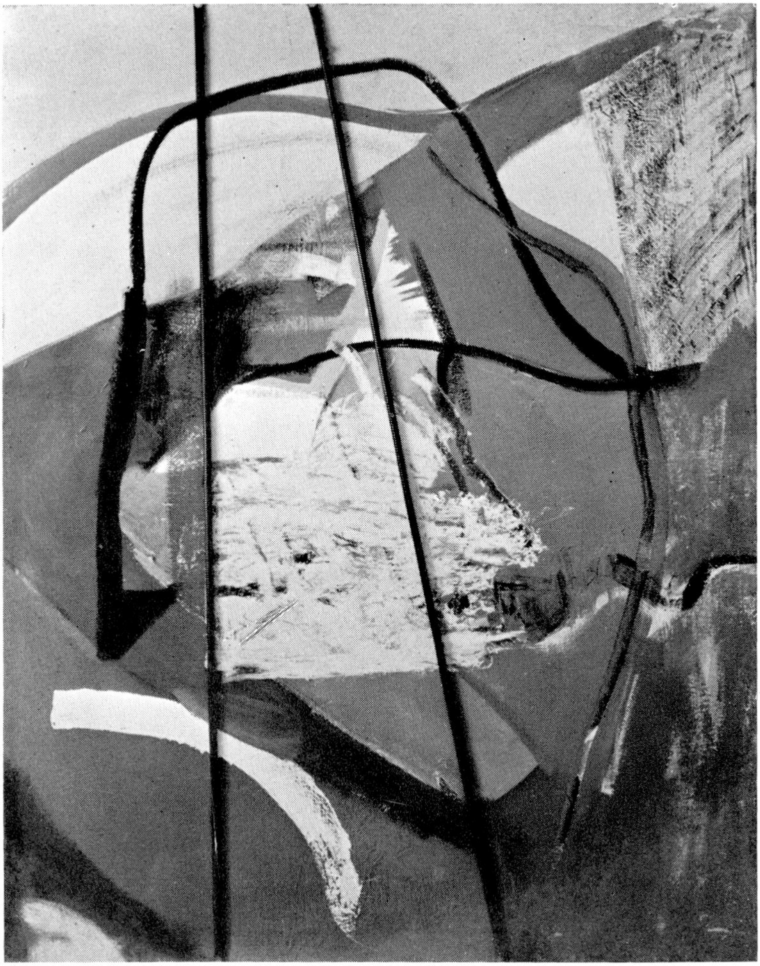

1 *Glide Path* (Peter Lanyon) (see p. 11)

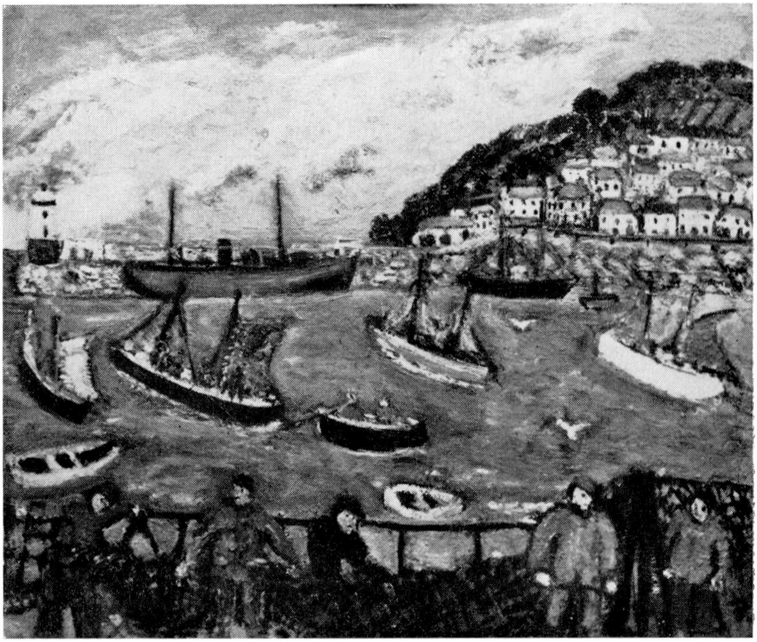

2 *Harbour* (Mary Jewells) (see p. 10)

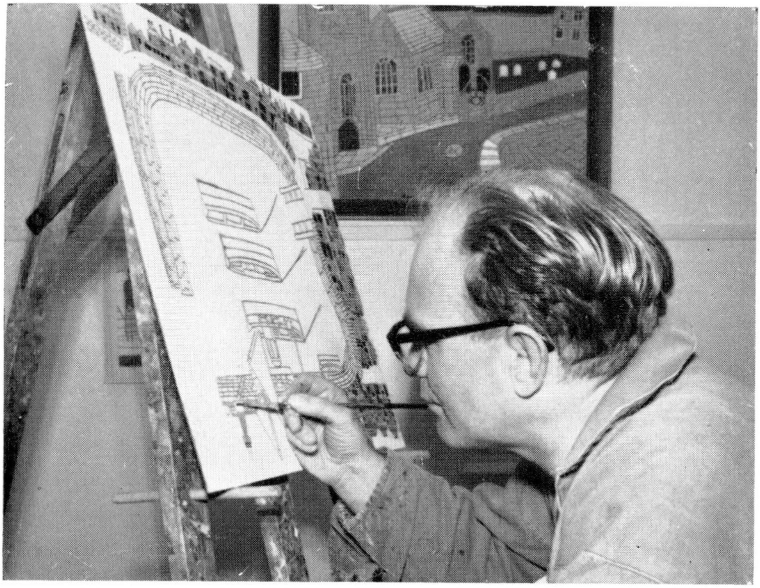

3 Bryan Pearce at Work

4 *Boats* (Bryan Pearce)

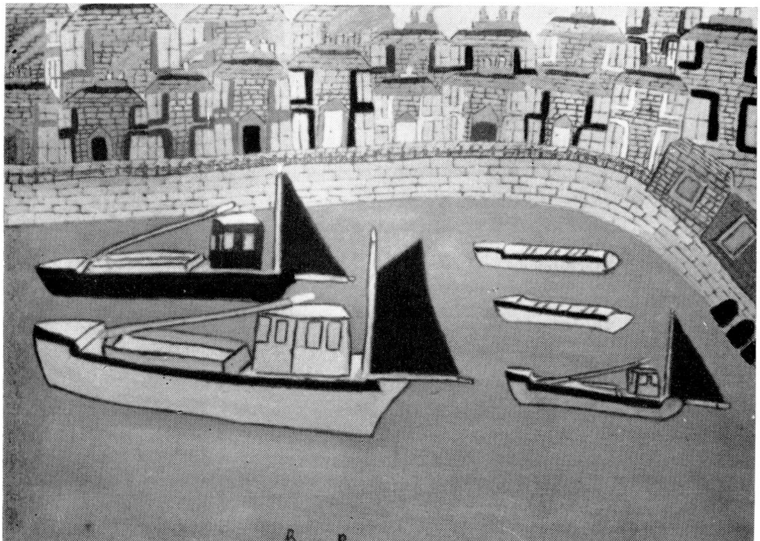

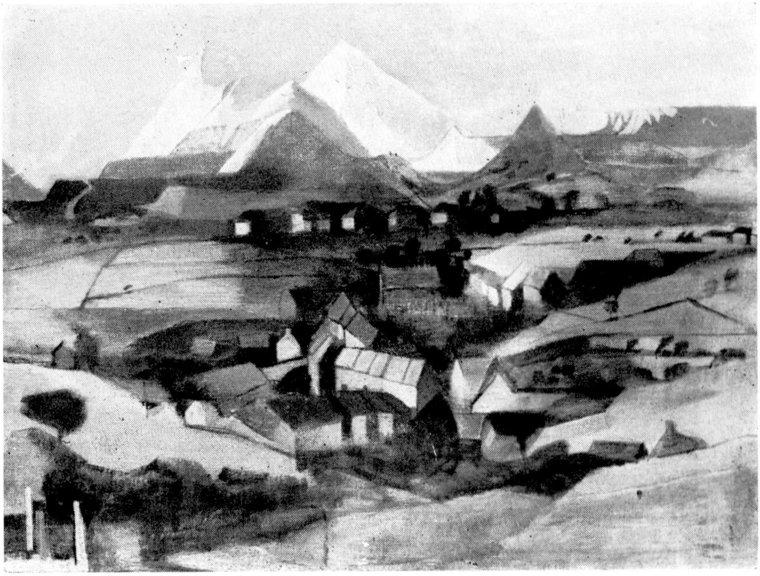

5 *Nanpean* (Ken Symonds)

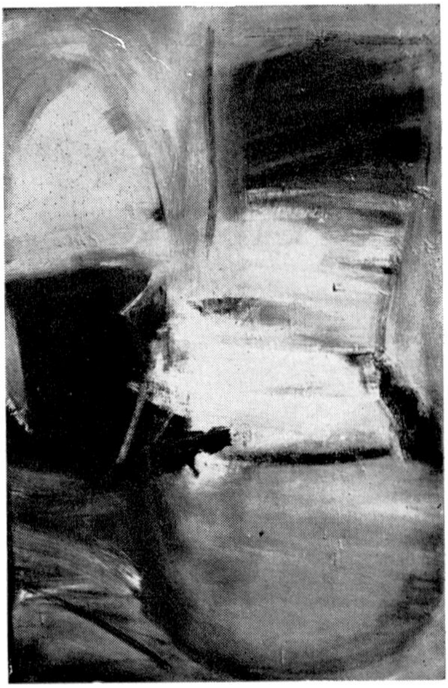

6 *Grey Dawn* (Dick Gilbert)
(see p. 12)

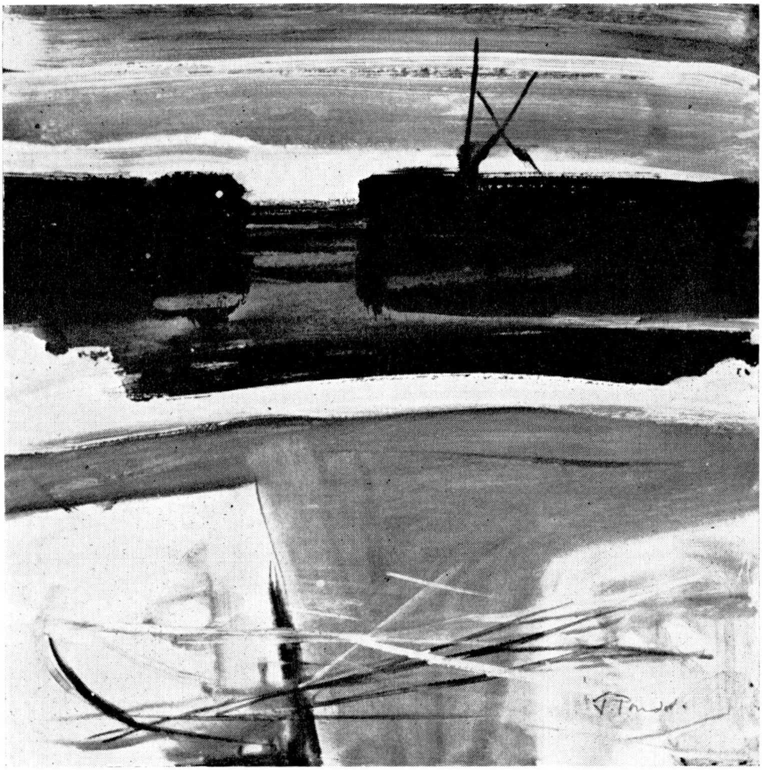

7 *Closed Harbour* (Jack Pender) (see pp. 14 and 15)

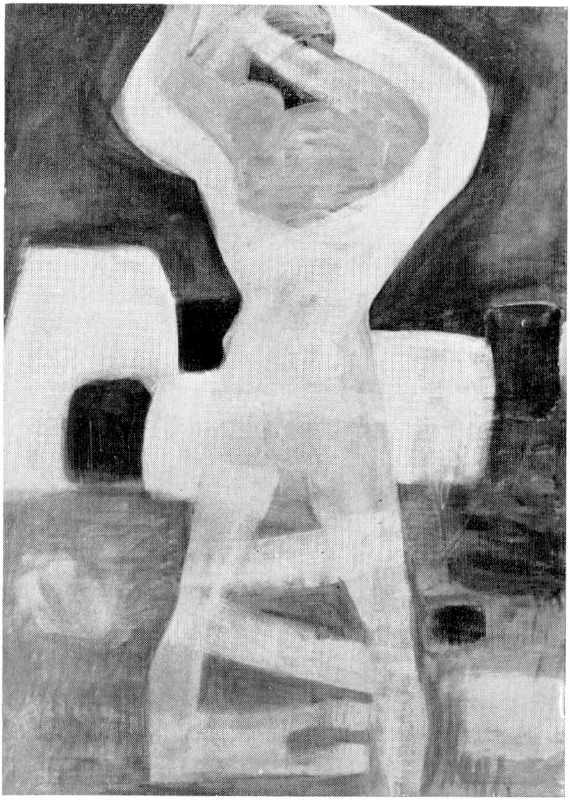

8 *Icarus* (John Miller)

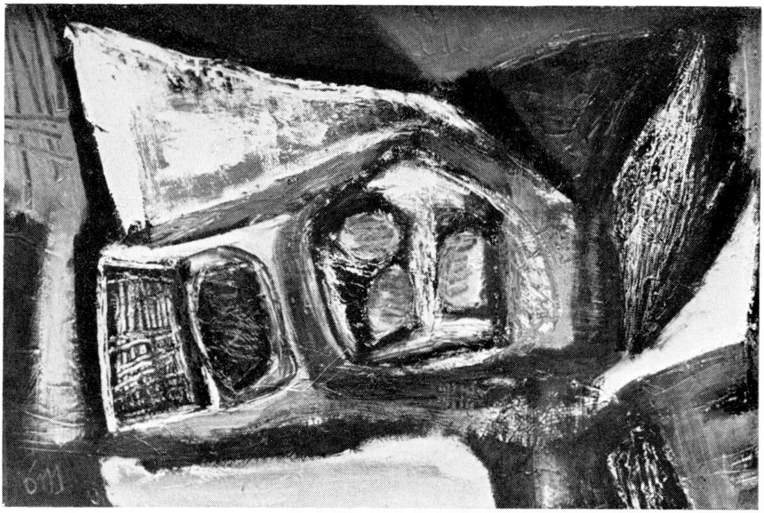

9 *Landscape* (Tony O'Malley)

10 *Ships* (Alfred Wallis)

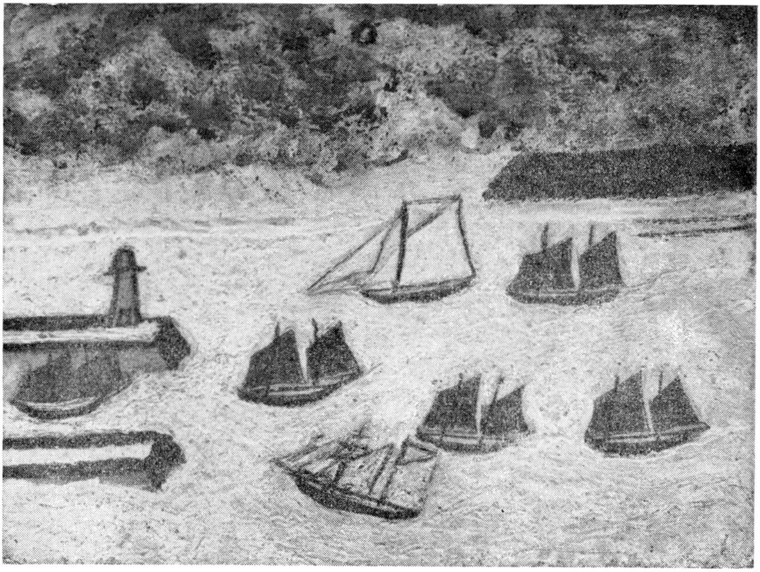

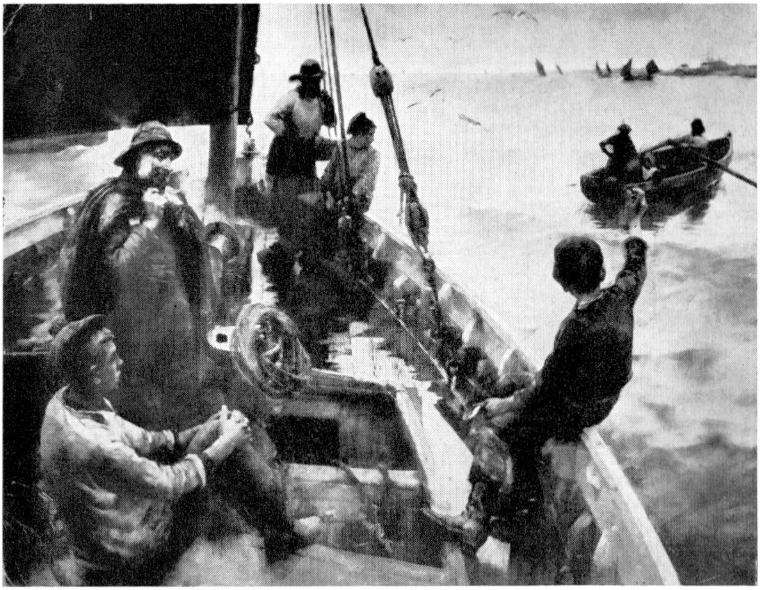

11 *Fishing Boats* (Stanhope Forbes) (see p. 17)

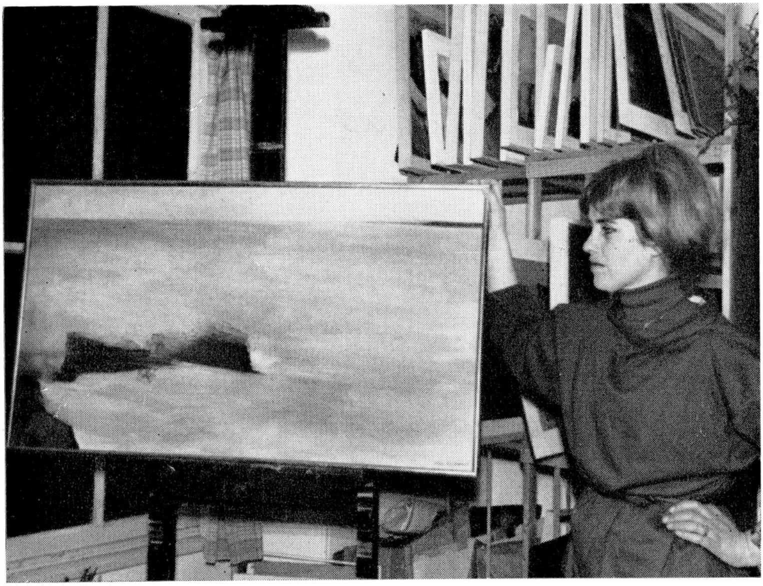

12 Margo Maeckleberghe at Work (see pp. 15 and 16)

13 *Newlyn* (Margo Maeckleberghe) (see pp. 15 and 16)

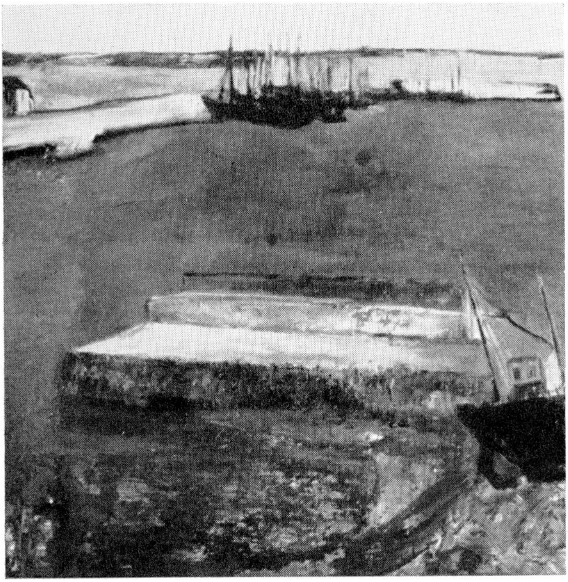

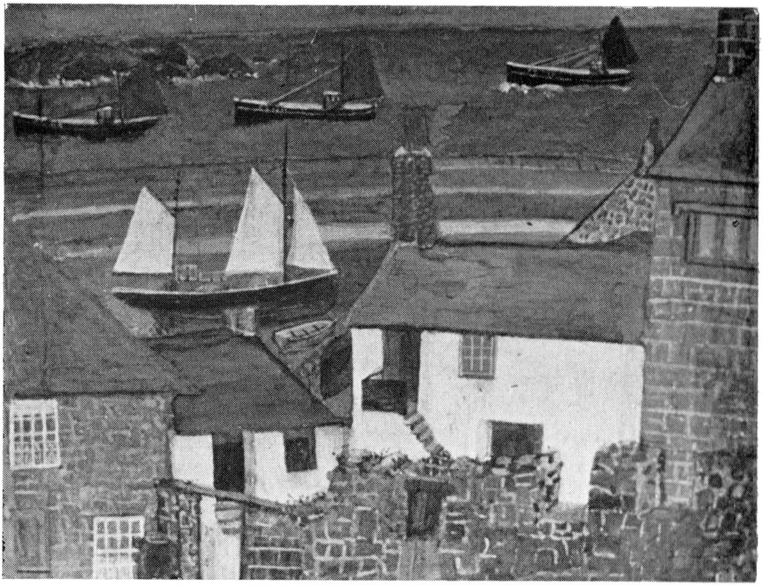

14 *Hurrying Boats* (W. George)

15 *Hayle Towan* (Misome Peile) (see p. 16)

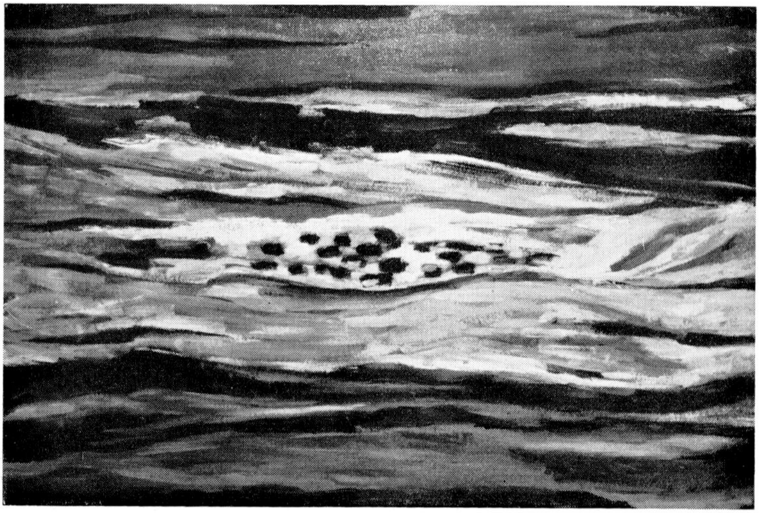

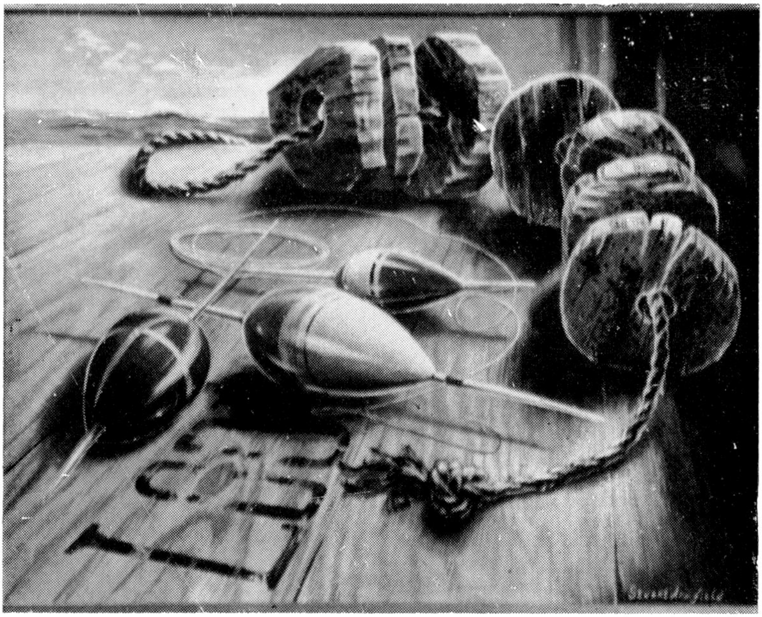

16 *Floats and Corks* (Stuart Armfield)

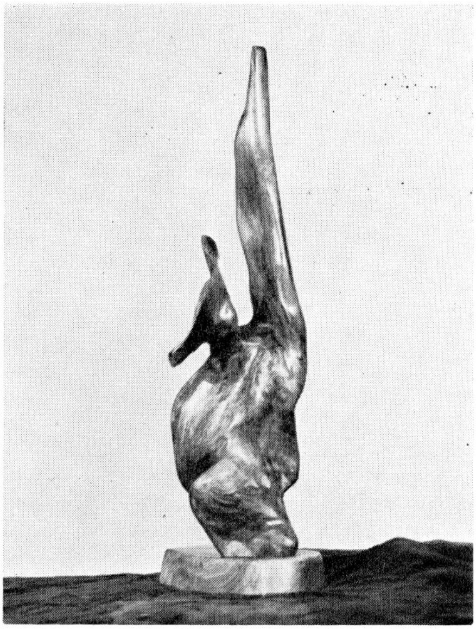

17 *Driftwood* (R. Cory)
(see p. 64)

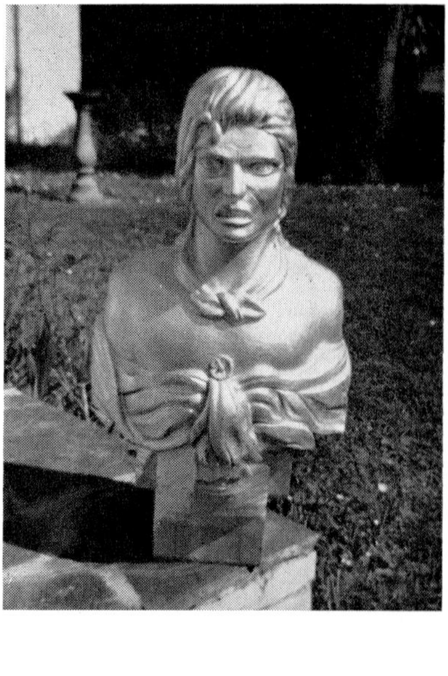

18 *Figurehead* (Charles Moore)

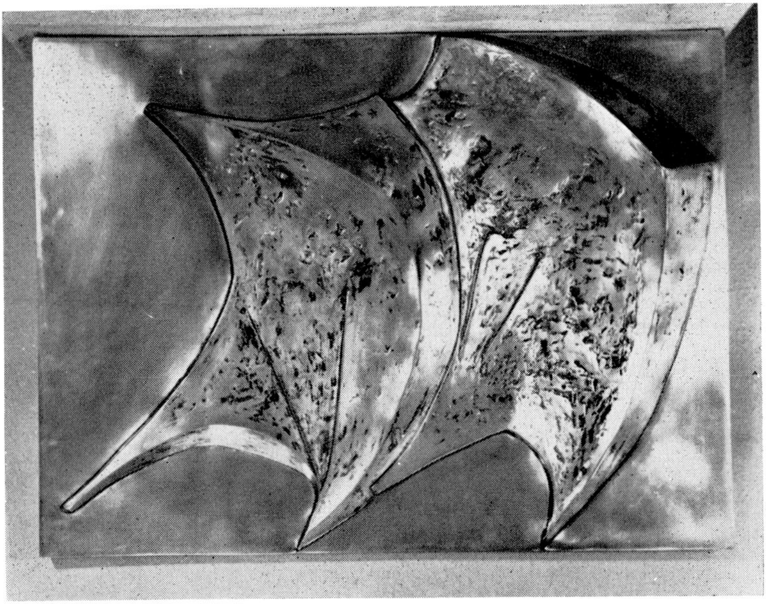

19 *Aluminium Relief* (John Milne)

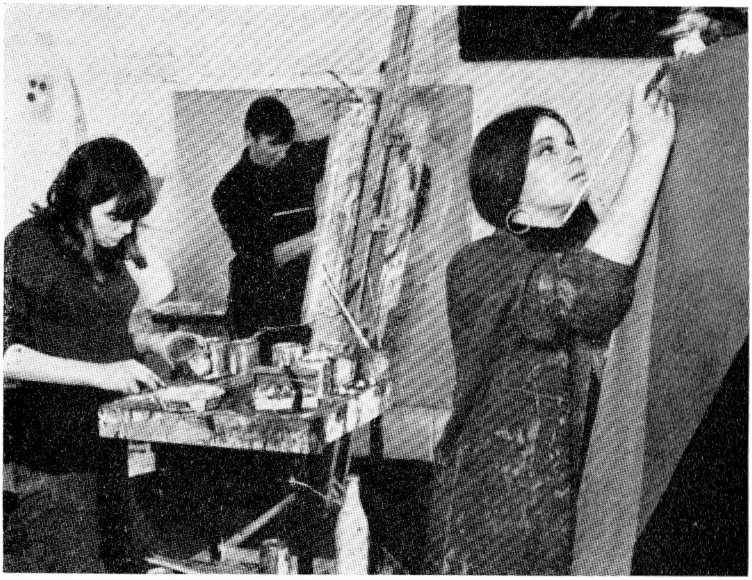

20 *Young Artists* (Falmouth Art School)

21 *Weaving* (Wyn Evans) (see pp. 65 and 66)

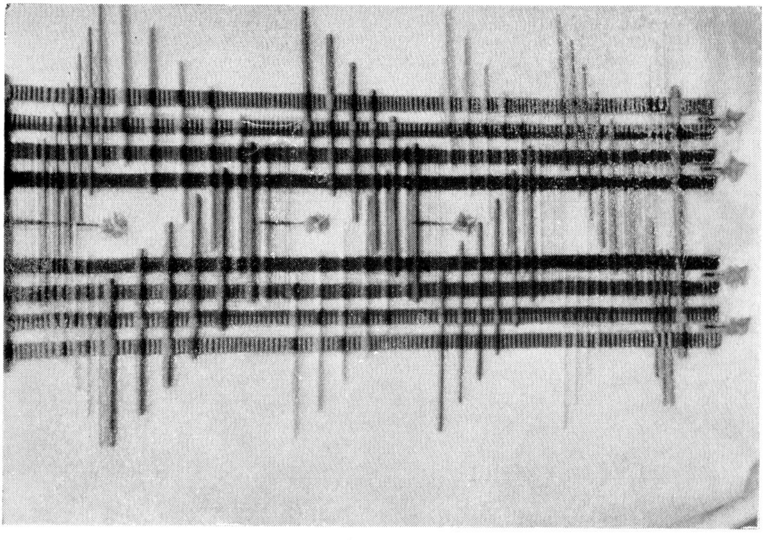

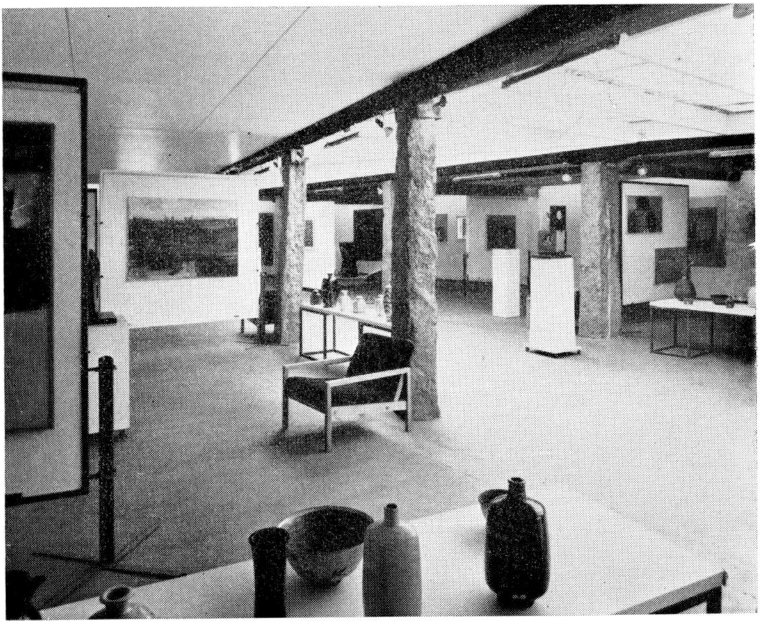

22 Penwith Gallery

23 Sheviock Gallery

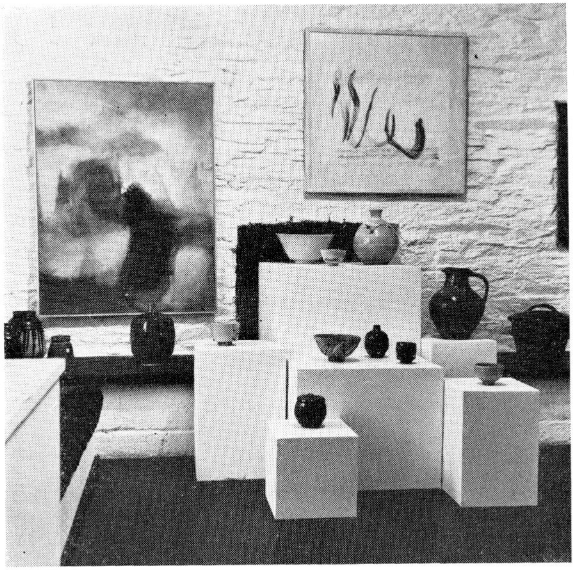

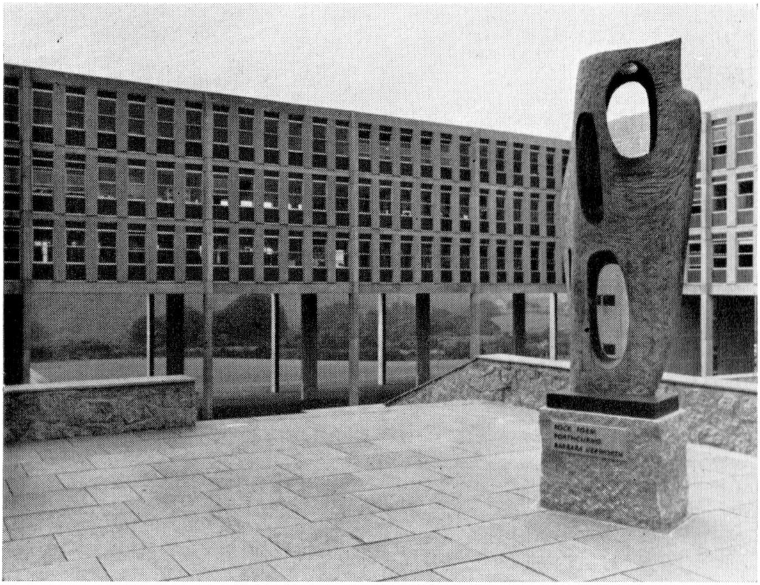

24 Barbara Hepworth Sculpture (see p. 14)

25 Bernard Leach and Pot (see pp. 68 and 69)

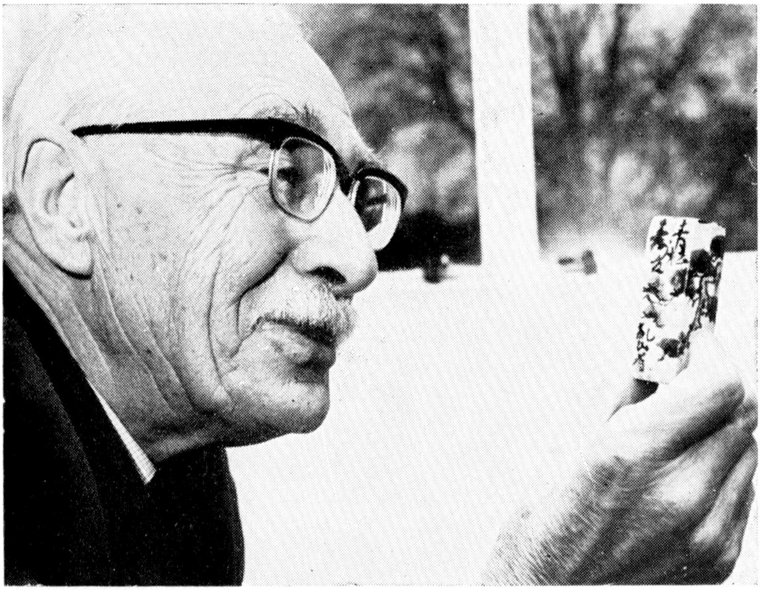

timidity, refer to the Cornish, the original British people, as 'English', could have learnt their mistake in Perran Round, as surely as those who persist in asserting that Cornish is dead. This play and entertainment were one sign among many that the Cornish language and spirit are far from extinct.

To conclude, one may I think, without blasphemy, appropriately quote from the play:

'Pan o marrow, dasserghys
Ve dhe Vewnans.'
('When it was dead, it was raised to life.')

Miss Charles mentioned the Helston Furry Dance. Along with its companion Spring celebration, the Padstow 'Obby' Oss, this forms what one might call Cornwall's most famous annual dramatic event. In recent years the Furry Dance has become a must for newspapers and the television companies, and it certainly makes a colourful spectacle, with dozens of couples, dolled up in their Sunday best, gravely pirouetting around in their perpetual dance to the strains of the Flora Dance. Now held on the first Saturday of May, Helston Flora Day attracts tens of thousands of visitors from all over the world: many of them, of course, Cornish exiles drawn back irresistibly by such a communal celebration —but many curious strangers as well, fascinated by this Festival rooted so pointedly in the past.

In recent years the Padstow affair has gained considerably in fame, and indeed is altogether a more spontaneous and—this is the important point—primitive event. At the Padstow celebrations it is impossible even for a 'foreigner' not to be strangely—I was going to write stirred, but the more correct word would be *disturbed*. All kinds of intimations and images of past ages are contained in the relentless, lurid—often sexual—motions of the 'Obby 'Oss as it writhes and shakes and shivers its way through the tiny streets. This, one feels, is something that is still linked with Cornwall's own very personal, very primitive past.

This same kind of atmosphere is sometimes captured—often fleetingly and unexpectedly, defying accurate charting—in the numerous other Feast Days held all over Cornwall. Helston and Padstow are only the two best known. There are many other very notable Feast Days which, for the town concerned are *the* days of the year. For some reason, which I often feel may be significant, most of these appear to take place in West Cornwall: in St Ives, Zennor, Marazion, and St Just. St Just Feast Day is a great occasion in that far-flung corner of the Cornish Empire. As at Helston and Padstow, thousands of people flock in for the day and though there are no longer the Bewnan Meryasek Plays at the round amphitheatre, as there would have been in the good old days, there are all kinds of special events, including a ceremonial football match between St Just and Plymouth Argyle. At night the five St Just pubs, miner's pubs basically, are crowded out and the merry-making goes on into the early hours.

Festivals are not the only public outlet for the Cornishman's love of the theatrical: carnivals are now ten-a-penny. I do not really know how common Carnivals are in other parts of Britain, but I have a shrewd suspicion they are somewhat peculiar to Cornwall. At any rate a Carnival in Cornwall is a big affair, to be taken very seriously. Local groups spend months in their preparations of the most intricate and ambitious floats, and the final processions sometimes last for six or seven hours. I remember in younger days driving a car for a large float in the annual Newlyn Carnival, when that affair took in a trip through the neighbouring towns of Mousehole and Penzance . . . my engine was boiling over by the time the enormous procession finally reached home again. I counted no fewer than 63 separate floats in that Carnival, and I have attended similar events at St Ives, at Falmouth, at Fowey, with equally impressive statistics. An interesting aspect of Carnivals is that they provide an opportunity for many sly (and broad!) digs at authority, or the raising of some long festering grievance about local conditions. Certainly there is more to them than first meets the eye, and to participate is a salutary experience.

Furry Dances, Festivals, Carnivals, lead us almost automatically to another Cornish theatrical event that goes back many hundreds of years for its origins: *Gorseth Kernow*. The revival of interest in the Cornish language, to which I referred in the opening chapter, has been paralleled by an enthusiastic revival of the old *Gorseths* (modelled in many ways on their more famous counterparts in Brittany and Wales). Appropriately enough the first of the revived *Gorseth Kernows* was held in 1928 at that magnificent memorial of past ages, the Bronze Age Circle of Boscawen-Un—the very spot where it is thought likely that 1000 years earlier the Bards of the whole Isle of Britain had gathered in a similar cermony. Since then the *Gorseths* have been held all over Cornwall, in spots varying from a dramatic setting by the Zennor moors to the centre of a town, Liskeard, on the busy A38 road (though on the site of a medieval castle). The objects of the *Gorseths* are to give expression to the national spirit of Cornwall: to encourage the study of Cornish history and the Cornish language, to foster Cornish literature, art and music; to link Cornwall with other Celtic countries; and to promote co-operation among those who work for the honour of Cornwall. Many of these aims are pursued all the year round through meetings and rallies, but inevitably the annual *Gorseth* is the *pièce de resistance*. There, at an impressive ceremony including crowning of the bards and various rituals spoken in old Cornish, a great deal of ancient drama is rekindled.

But what of the future? G. Pawley White, an immediate Past Grand Bard, has considered this question:

> Have the flowing blue robes, the sounds of the Corn Gwlas and the harp and the ceremonies conducted in a once-defunct language any place in the 'seventies? The robes, as do academic robes, certainly play a picturesque and colourful part in the ceremonies, the sounds of horn and harp are more pleasant than many of the sounds which afflict our ears elsewhere, and the language is recognised as an essential part of the Cornish heritage. There will always be a place in the life of the community for the beauty and colour of pageantry and spectacle. The real work of the College of Bards, however, is done not at the Open Gorseth for everyone to see 'in the eye of the sun,' but in the continuing work of the members in the various organisations they serve. Much of their enthusiasm will continue to come from their association with other workers in the Gorseth, which, through its Council, can give a lead to public opinion in matters affecting Cornish life. In these days when the importance of nations, governments, industries and organisations is judged by sheer size, the peculiar treasures that minorities can contribute to the Commonwealth tend to be forgotten. It is through such activities as those of the College of Bards that regional individuality may be preserved and fostered, so that we are not all reduced to a dull uniformity. Gorseth Kernow will continue to foster the progress of the culture of Cornwall, to enrich the common life by the development of resources latent in the Cornish people and to encourage peace and friendship amongst all people. Thus in the seventh decade of the twentieth century would it fulfil its watchwords of *Kernow, Cres ha Kerensa*—Cornwall, Peace and Friendship.

I have stressed the theatrical nature of such events as the Furry Dance, the 'Obby 'Oss, Carnivals and Festivals, and the Cornish *Gorseth*, because they are all peculiar to the county of the origin. After all, there is no Devon *Gorseth*, or Berkshire *Gorseth*, and the idea is somehow unthinkable: equally the Furry Dance and the 'Obby 'Oss just could not be transferred to any other part of England. So we see that these events belong, dramatically, to the Cornish way of life . . . and as such they have often a profound effect upon the people living and working in Cornwall.

When we turn to drama, as it is more conventionally understood, that is, drama in the form of professional theatre, we find a paucity of it in the county. Over the years various attempts have been made to bring professional theatre to Cornwall, and there have been repertory companies at Penzance, at Perranporth, at Falmouth, but they have all failed after a short period. The reason for this is the obvious one that the Cornish prefer their own amateur theatricals: many hundreds, perhaps 1000 or more, will attend some popular performance by the

Redruth Operatic Society or the Truro Society or the West Cornwall Theatre Group—whereas I can remember, during a period when I assisted the Avon Players, a professional company based in Falmouth, often playing to houses of 20 or less.

Perhaps significantly the one sphere in which drama *has* flourished in Cornwall has been the open-air theatre—and in particular one special open-air theatre, the Minack, that unique area carved out of the granite cliffs at Porthcurno, just east of Land's End. Here in a setting of true mystery and grandeur an audience would find it difficult not to be intrigued, indeed overwhelmed, by the sheer physical drama of the occasion. On the occasion of a typical Minack performance on a fine summer evening the single road leading down to Porthcurno and approached either *via* Sennen or Treen is crowded with cars and motor-coaches bringing eager parties of theatre-lovers. Many more people walk along the lanes, or take short cuts across fields, or follow the beautiful coastal paths. Everyone is going in the same direction; everyone sooner or later passes by the tiny stone box-office and follows the winding gravel path that leads inexorably down and down. Now, indeed, the sea stretches towards the infinite horizon, making a unique and perfect backcloth. But all attention is directed nearer at hand—to the lovely stretch of greensward bounded by natural granite boulders on the east and west and (even more dramatically) by the man-made balustrades and walls, and a great throne along the southern edge. Row by row, the wise ones bearing blankets and other protective clothing against possible squalls, the audience assembles around the semi-circle of tiers of grass seats. There is no curtain, but perhaps a trumpet sounds, or a herald's voice is heard, and the first players appear, decked in richly coloured garments. The play begins . . .

Nora Ratcliff, the first playwright to be commissioned to write a play for the Minack, has some interesting reminiscences:

> The theatre haunted me. Again and again and again we came back to a discussion of the plays to be done and I found myself dissatisfied not with the plays themselves, but with the fact that they didn't fit the theatre. The Minack demanded its own play. Whatever play was put on the Atlantic would be the main factor . . .

Finally it was agreed that Mrs Ratcliff should write her own version of the *Tristan & Iseult* legend.

> Looking back the rest seems to have been comparatively simple. I read up the material with the Minack in mind: anything that didn't fit automatically dropped out of recollection. My imagination was chiefly caught by the 'theatre' of the scene where Mark hands Iseult down to the Lepers. As I read I saw Iseult

moving slowly down from the top gate . . . a half-mad Mark stared up at her; grey, lichen-like shales of lepers lay on the rocks to the audience's left. Obviously the long wall over to the right became Mark's inner castle; the entrance from the harbour had to be up the steps on the right—and so on. Scene after scene unfolded itself; all that remained was to write it.

Thanks to the kindness of Miss Cade, owner of the Minack, I was able to go down to the Minack and stay there with nothing to do but write. . . . The play couldn't have been written anywhere else but at the Minack: not only so that that one could check the staging but so that the sea, the gulls, the changing light could find their way into the imagery of the play itself: tilted wing of a gull, black as a rock's shadow, torn through the rock teeth . . .

Subsequently Mrs Ratcliff not only produced the play but joined the Chorus and tasted the play from the stage itself:

I shall never regret having done so: the joy of playing on the Minack stage, of feeling a part of the total effect, sensing the attention of the audience (even hearing the screwing back of thermos flask tops as a new scene opened) was a high reward for wearing a scratchy hessian frock and scrambling down to the dressing tent over rocky paths in the uncertain flicker of storm lanterns.

At one of the early rehearsals with the Minack cast some bright spirit suggested a 'midnight matinee', and the idea grew to resolution. It didn't matter if nobody came. We wanted to play the whole thing in stage lighting—perhaps that was the reason, or perhaps we knew that by the last night we should be so Minack-drunk that to leave the theatre at 10.30 would be an anti-climax. So the midnight matinee was launched; to start at 11 p.m., less than an hour after the normal performance had ended. It seemed to us as we waited for the first horn-call, that half Cornwall wanted to see a play at midnight; if, as someone said, we were mad, then the entire Penwith peninsula was peopled with lunatics! A black, lava-like stream of audience oozed down the treacherous path; pale blue programmes twinkled under pocket torches: a full moon—perhaps that explained things—glimmered on white head-dresses of the players; fringes of white foam sighed round the Minack Rock. Second horn-call: we each clutched our cheese, our salmon, basket of eggs, and the last performance of *Tristan of Cornwall* started. It was then I knew that for at least fifty people scattered about the shadowy rocks, the Minack Theatre, an immortal love story, and the warmth of friendship engendered by mutual creation, would be inextricably interwoven in a lasting memory. Thank you, Cornwall.

Since then Minack has been the setting for many notable performances —including *King Lear, Othello*, Shaw's *Caesar and Cleopatra*, Christopher Fry's *The Firstborn* and Norman Nicholson's *Prophecy to the Wind*—as well as several more specifically Cornish plays by Nora Ratcliff. Whatever the play, or the performance, it is the setting that dominates and imposes a curious and indeed unique influence. Drama at the Minack is unlike drama anywhere else in Britain!

Many of the plays performed at the Minack have also been put on at other open-air theatres in Cornwall—of which the most prominent are

Perran Round, near Perranporth, Gwennap Pit, at Redruth, and the grounds of Restormel Castle, above Lostwithiel. Certainly open-air drama seems right for Cornwall and this in a way is further evidence of the importance of the physical background in this county.

Cornish playwrights, it appears, have we none—unless one counts the poet Ronald Duncan who has written several verse dramas, such as *This Way to the Tomb*, though none has been set in Cornwall. But oddly enough, at various times there has been quite a vogue for playwrights to cash in on the instinctive public tendency to equate Cornwall with a truly dramatic situation and setting. Drama critic, J.C. Trewin, himself a sturdy Cornishman *Up from the Lizard*, to use the title of his autobiography, once wrote an amusing article 'Pins in the Images', describing how he had made a lifelong hobby of collecting commercial plays about Cornwall—nearly all of them very melodramatic, few memorable. As it seemed to Trewin, 'Melodrama; Cornwall,' the words chimed together. Among the plays he had collected it was noticeable that:

> Cliffs, mines and lighthouses were all uncommonly useful; among these we gather, Cornish people made what precarious living they could. Matters had been almost as bad in the eighteenth century. Then you rarely went to Cornwall by normal means; you were wrecked there on a coast that drew vessels to it like needles to a loadstone. Set out for Portugal and you would land—with luck—on a drifting spar at Porthcurno.

Among his collection Mr Trewin refers to two recent plays which their authors obviously felt to be truly atmospherical and full of local colour.

> One, set in West Penwith, contained a malignant witch woman, an aged mother-in-law who raised storms; we had also a death by drowning and a fall from a cliff. I felt we had slipped into the Middle Ages and were being shown round, anachronistically, by a student of Synge with no ear for the rhythms. Another piece, even worse, contained a housekeeper who jabbed pins into waxen images and a victim who was throttled in a mine near Land's End. It was this that made me reflect upon neo-Cornish drama as a set of variations on the world gloom; boom, loom, doom, tomb.

Not one of these plays was written by a Cornish writer, of course. However, in the allied field of opera, Cornwall has produced some composers—notably George Lloyd, Inglis Gundry, and Philip Cannon. The first opera to be written in this generation by a Cornishman turned to the old myths of the land: it was '*Iernin*' written by George Lloyd with a libretto by his father, William. The Lloyds lived in Zennor and young George grew up with Cornwall in his blood, so it was hardly surprising he should choose as his theme the local legend of the Nine Maidens, that great circle of granite boulders near Land's End—the maidens having been turned into stone for dancing on a Sunday.

Inglis Gundry, a Cornish bard who has devoted most of his life to the study of Cornish music and language, has tapped a rich vein of Cornish lore for his operas. *The Tinners of Cornwall* is, as its title suggests, about the early miners; *The Logan Rock*, actually written for the Minack Theatre, is an attempt to recreate the old Cornish 'drolls' which used to be enacted in earlier times at the open-air round theatres.

Philip Cannon, the third of the Cornish operatists, whose opera *Morvoren* was recently produced in London, wrote of it in an article in *Musical Times*:

> Opera has been in my mind ever since I was a boy in Cornwall. The Cornish half of me wanted to reveal in musical terms the fascinating hinterland where truth and legend meet, where the ancient culture and superstitions of Cornwall would appear against their true background of ruggedly beautiful coast line and wilder sea. It was this inner life, the musical inflection of Cornish speech, I felt I could set to music.

Maisie Radford, who wrote the libretto for the opera, has this to say:

> The underlying theme the hidden conflict which is the life of opera, was the contrast in the Cornish character: the home-loving, chapel-going life with something wilder and more primitive which comes of being always up against the elements, the sea and the hard life of the sea. With this in mind it seemed that the story of Morvoren, or the Mermaid, offered the perfect theme.
>
> There are many legends of mermaids to be found around the Cornish coast, of which the story of the Mermaid of Zennor, associated as it is with the carving of the mermaid on the pew-end in the church, is the best known. The stories usually take roughly the same form: the beautiful unknown maiden who comes to the village, is eventually drawn back to her true home in the sea, taking with her the young man who has fallen in love with her. In *Morvoren*, the first scene is set in a Wesleyan School Room. Preparations for a Harvest Festival are going on and the Preacher puts an end to the bustle and gossip by calling on the villagers to conclude with a hymn for those at sea—'and this young lady shall lead the singing'. Morvoren begins, shyly at first and keeping to the notes of the hymn. In the last verse she sings a strange tune above the hymn, changing its whole character. The hymn ends, but she is carried away by her song and goes on singing—unconscious of what she is doing. Philip Cannon fully realised this contrast in his music; the broad confident four-part hymn tune and the wayward chromatic free-ranging line of Morvoren's singing strike at once the heart of the situation, and foreshadow the conflict in the heart of Matthey, the young fisherman, which is to lead to his tragedy. This strange character in Morvoren's music is kept throughout, only becoming more human in her love scene with Matthey, tho' even here Cannon has described the music as 'Passionate imitation which never quite meets either rhythmically or harmonically.'

The preacher, stable and sensible but narrowly determined to shield his flock from strange imaginings; Thirza, the old seaweed gatherer who alone suspects Morvoren's strange origin, the old Huer, who keeps the look out for the shoals of fish and whose call was directly taken from the actual cry as demonstrated by a St Ives fisherman, were all strongly characterised. We determined from the first to set the scene no further back than the turn of the Century, and to use dialect only in so far as the Cornish turn of speech and the vivid expressions and occasional dialect words could be heard today among the older people, and had indeed been heard by ourselves in our daily contacts.

Cannon made a careful study in his recitatives of the inflexions of Cornish speech—in particular the rise at the end of a sentence which is common in Celtic voices. The choruses of fishermen going down to the boats and the gossip of women gave ample opportunity to the chorus. The final scene, in which Matthey is drowned and all the warring elements—the storm at sea, the voices of the unseen chorus of mermaids, and the hymn tune by which the preacher tries to rally the frightened villagers—are combined, swelling to a fine climax.

From opera it is a natural step to music, in the drama scale.

To live in Cornwall is to live in the midst of music. Nothing comparable can be heard in the neighbouring counties, yet they too are largely rural, lacking big towns and facilities for large scale entertainment. Why was this tradition of musicality established and how is it faring today?

The background can only be briefly suggested; the Celtic blood; the pattern of life associated with mining, frequently leaning to a strong tradition of choral singing; the religious revival, working in a people oppressed by economic and climatic hardship—and having a musical expression similar in its fervour to that of the oppressed negroes in the southern states of the U.S.A., and the isolated rural community life of earlier times.

Joy McMullen, director of the Cornwall Rural Music School, made those comments once when she explained how widespread musicality —not considered a preserve of the comfortable middle classes—has been the special mark of Cornish music-making:

Brass bands and small orchestras sprang up in the smallest village community. Even today you will find villages where one family can supply enough musicians for all festive occasions, religious and secular. Singers formed not only church choirs and male voice choirs but in the town, operatic and choral societies. Talk to any one of these old school vocalists and they will describe how they worked many extra hours in the evenings, so they might make enough money to pay to travel frequently long distances by train, catching the "Workmen's Special" early in the morning, to have their much-prized individual tuition—perhaps once a week, but more likely once a month, since fees could be anything up to a guinea even fifty years ago. String players, too, will tell you how, as a youngster, one of them would have the violin lesson and run home to his friend's back kitchen, to pass on the latest advance skill—like a saffron bun hot from the oven. Instruments in those days had to be bought outright, and again meant months and years of hard work and saving.

All that happened 50 years ago, and more. What goes on today? Musical life still flourishes, but perhaps with a change of emphasis. Probably less children learn the piano, but more take up brass and stringed instruments, and get to a higher standard, with more opportunities to play. Other instruments—mainly orchestral woodwind and brass—are available. For the adult, there are bands, orchestras, choirs and operatic societies. Every sizable town has both a choral and an operatic society, as well as its numerous church and chapel choirs. All this activity represents the work of small, local bodies; of the Brass Band Association; the Local Education Authority, and the Cornwall Rural Music School.

Cornish ways may change, the land remains the same: that narrow, elongated lobster-claw still stretches westward into the sea. Few people have the means or time to travel more than perhaps 10 miles for leisure pursuits and this means—in a county this shape—that centres for leisure activities must be scattered over a wide area. The Rural Music School has to provide *peripatetic* tuition and music-making. It is, like Tudor royalty, a 'movable feast,' progressing round the country, complete with its own regalia of timp sticks and music stands. Every July, for instance, the school removes itself from its work-a-day base to the beautiful St Mylor Church, near Flushing. Here it gives a festival of evening concerts of seventeenth-and eighteenth- century music, blending choral and instrumental, professional and amateur, in a varied, often unusual, programme of music with something to delight every ear. This event comes annually at the end of a hard year's teaching work, in which staff have covered several hundreds of miles. Tuition centres at present cover central Cornwall: Falmouth, Helston, Truro, St. Austell and Bodmin. The orchestral meetings draw people from Penzance, up to Bude, and Liskeard, and can really be said to serve the whole county, but tuition cannot yet be offered so widely. The dichotomy of high teaching standards and reasonably low fees is schizophrenic enough; to add heavy expenditure in travelling would be suicidal. In conjunction with the L.E.A. the C.R.M.S. is responsible for string class teaching in Central Cornwall, and this has been a further factor in the school's development.

The music festivals that Mrs McMullen mentions are only a few among many. Every year, in all kinds of remote corners of Cornwall, quite imposing festivals are held—like that at St Endemellion Church in North Cornwall, to which musicians from 'up country' come for a whole week of performances. Another unusual festival is the Porth-en-Alls Music Festival held in a private house at Prussia Cove, Perranuthnoe—the house being built into the side of the cliff, with the front door on the top floor and the lowest floor, three landings below, standing on the rocks on which the sea breaks.

When we arrived, one day before the final concert in Penzance, the orchestra was rehearsing in one room, the choir in another, and the children were running their own orchestra in a third. I mention the children because this festival is very much a family affair. All the houses on the estate were occupied by families, all of whom took part in the music, singing, playing or both. About half were amateurs, some of whom had travelled from as far as Liverpool, but many were natives of Penzance, Newlyn or Mousehole. The other half were professionals, amongst whom was Ilse Wolf, who still love music enough to come to this house for a week to make music with us amateurs just for the enjoyment. The keynote was enjoyment, though, under the baton of Roger Norrington, a remarkably high standard was demanded and achieved. Everybody joined in something, and hardly anybody was unemployed. One of the horn players was really a trombonist, and this was only the third time he had played a horn in our orchestra; no mean feat in Stravinsky's Dumbarton Oaks Concerto, and very well he played it, too. The other horn player, Michael Behrens, is the owner of the estate. He is a sheep farmer, who had 450 new-born lambs to nurse single-handed, which created a sitting-in problem far greater than that of the many parents taking part in the music. His brother, a violin teacher, was in the first desk of the violins, which were led by Penelope Howard. His sister-in-law, Alison Gordon, played the solo part in Mozart's A major Piano Concerto in the concert at Penzance. It was a lovely performance, particularly in the slow movement, which was played at the most sustained and serene pace, while the last movement bubbled along with a gaiety and lightness of touch I have seldom heard before. After the Concerto she joined the choir and sang in the Mozart C minor Mass. Most of the orchestra sang in two unaccompanied Stravinsky motets. A surgeon from Liverpool played the clarinet in the piano concerto and then sang the tenor solo in the Mass. His wife played the violin and the viola in the orchestra, and led an informal performance, late one evening in front of a log fire, of the Mozart Clarinet Quintet.

In the evenings, after supper, one could usually hear the sound of madrigals or chamber music coming from cottages all over the estate. When the Quintet was over, we tried, rather unsuccessfully, to sight-read some Gesualdo, ending after midnight, with better renderings of some Pilkington and Vantor.

That account by Anthony Gillingham in the CORNISH REVIEW of a week at the Porth-en-Alls Festival—gives a tiny personal flavour of experiences to be found even to this day in Cornwall in which the setting is, as ever, a vital part of the experience. Instrumental music in the low-beamed sitting-room of some Elizabethan Cornish house—choir singing in the ancient granite hall of a sixteenth century church—brass-band music blaring out in the narrow cobbled street of a china-clay village like Bugle, up among the 'white mountains'—or simply the dancing lilt of the Helston Flora Dance as it moves round and round the streets of that old market town—these are all part of a world of drama and music and song peculiar to Cornwall.

VII

Crafts of Cornwall

CRAFTSMANSHIP has been described as the gradual transfer of the bodily knowledge of the right usages of material and the intimate co-operation of small groups of workers. If the continuity is broken and the workers and their materials split up, then not only is a craft lost, but a whole heritage. During World War II when nearly all crafts except purely rural ones came to a standstill there was a very real danger of British craftsmenship suffering a mortal blow: fortunately this was averted and one of the most encouraging developments since has been the tremendous revival of interest in crafts.

Nowhere has this been more striking than in Cornwall where, according to a survey by the Rural Industries Bureau, there are nearly 400 *separate* crafts in existence in the county. Some of these, such as the painting of sea-shells and the making of fancy jewellery and decorations from pebble stones, are somewhat superficial and intended solely for the tourist trade. But most of the crafts practised in Cornwall are very old and very traditional—those of the blacksmith, the wheelright, the saddler, the potter. Among exponents of these crafts are some of the best known members of their profession not only in Cornwall but in the country: Bernard Leach, potter; Francis Cargeeg, coppersmith; Robin Nance, furniture-maker; the late Percy Mitchell, boat-builder. Pioneers such as these inevitably drew their followers, who in turn encourage others, and so whole crafts movements are built up.

In Cornwall, too, there is the important link with the Celtic past. Francis Cargeeg has put it like this:

> The significance of any art is illuminated alike by its history and the approach to it by the artist. This is especially true of the art of hand beaten copper, and as my approach to it has been so deeply influenced by its historical and archaeological associations, that aspect of my craft inevitably introduces my subject. The data of archaeology is a history of art, and in its creative reaching out towards 'new' modes of expression, shows that modern art has paradoxically groped its way into the realm of archaeology, and odd, shadowy forms have long haunted the studios of the Western world. Shades of the artist-craftsmen who wrought the Neolithic figurines, the Benin bronzes and Negro

wood-carvings, the Inca pottery, the strange Maya art, and indeed everywhere and in every medium have given visual significance to the ritual of birth, life and death. Somewhere in the shadows are the master-craftsmen of the ancient Celtic world who bequeathed to us such treasures as the Battersea shield, the mirrors of Desborough and St Keverne, the Ardagh chalice and the Tara brooch.

A curious, almost instinctive interest in their work grew out of the love of a Cornish Celt for his country and its history, a history that can only be understood in its relationship to the immense field of Celtic history and archaeology in general. And the key to that understanding lies in the rich legacy of Celtic art, the creativity of a race whose dominion stretched for a thousand years from the Black Sea to the western coast of Ireland. Its artists in pottery, weaving, metal-work, enamelling, ecclesiastical stonework and illuminated manuscript gave to Europe a masterly abstract art of curvilinear and geometric ornament. They excelled, however, in metal-work, and in hammered sheet bronze, which is copper with a little tin added, they found a medium that perfectly suited their instincts and achieved astonishing results in the technique of 'embossing' designs which we now know as 'repoussé'.

Their designs were drawn by the flow of light on polished metal, which gave an elusive beauty to their oft-times flamboyant and bizarre forms. My interests thus led inevitably to Celtic metalwork and to hammered copper as an ideal medium to interpret the spirit which lived in the scrolls, the spiral and trumpet motifs and the amazing patterns of knot work so beloved by the ancient artist craftsmen.

My interests went hand in hand with a certain artistic urge which sent me to an art school in the evenings and to the open air with easel and water colours whenever possible. In this pilgrimage a dream slowly took shape of devoting myself to the awakening of interest in Celtic art and to restoring the prestige of beaten copper as an art-form. The interest in Celtic art in the antiquarian coteries in Cornwall was almost nil, and the art schools a subject for distinctly 'sniffy' comments: whilst owing to the ease with which copper can be manipulated by the machine, the once lovely art of beaten copper had become degraded to the point of extinction and served but to brighten the ironmongery department and solve the problems of the seaside souvenir hunters. So I left the security of an engineering job up-country, crossed the Tamar into my native land, and set myself the task of literally hammering out a new pattern of life and making a distinct contribution to the Celtic revival of Cornwall.

Francis Cargeeg concludes a thoughtful resumé of his life-work (he is now an octogenarian) with these words:

My tribute has been by hand, hammer and fire to try to make a living reality of a great traditional art. My experience has brought me an acute sense of fellowship with my forerunners, and a satisfaction in sharing in the significant and inevitable revival of the crafts. Significant because it is part of that questing for those basic aesthetic values which, hag-ridden by the analytical spirit of a scientific age, the artist bewilderingly seeks. Inevitable because all they seek has been part of the way of life, labour and thought of artist craftsmen since the dawn-cultures of mankind. Hence the haunting of the studios, the hopeful drawing together of the artist and the craftsman, and the emergence of the artist craftsman of a new age.

Francis Cargeeg refers to what has been encouragingly evident in recent years, a real craft 'explosion' in Cornwall. Just as we can trace, sometimes further back in time, a significant movement of painters and poets and writers in Cornwall, so today there is much evidence of the same trend among craftsmen. Of course, there are certain geographic factors which would apply to all remote country areas—e.g. the Highlands of Scotland, Wales, Ireland—all of which draw craft workers, too (though not on the same concentrated scale). But the same *extra* features which have drawn other artists to Cornwall have applied to the craftsmen, too —the surging sea, the white-washed sands, the craggy cliffs, the desolate moors, the haunted interiors.

R.H. Cory, who from his home at Widemouth, near Bude, has developed an unusual driftwood craft, lectures entertainingly to various Cornish societies on his experiences:

To those of us fortunate enough to have been born in the vicinity of the North Cornish coast probably nothing developed more naturally or spontaneously than the leisure-time occupation of beachcombing. It therefore seemed natural that when I retired I should concentrate on developing shapes from driftwood. This seemed to me an ideal medium by which to express that inherent artistic urge, the expression of which enriches life—the medium costs nothing except the labour required to collect it. Practical experience has deepened my fascination in the craft, giving me new concepts and insights as well as providing problems and challenges. I became increasingly interested in the sources of the wood, the changes which took place in certain woods exposed to the action of sea water over a long period, and the relation of winds, currents and tides to the supplies of the raw material I needed.

The techniques used to develop shapes from driftwood are matters of individual choice, as is the preference for tools. My own methods are essentially simple. I remove all bark, soft and rotted surface and faulty pieces by using files, chisels and a coping saw. There then remains the basic wood, which is obviously different in shape from the original piece. At this stage decision has to be made as to the ultimate shape required, so imagination and artistic sense come into play. The wood is viewed from all angles, regard being given to the grain and pattern and how they follow the curves, and account is taken of hollows and cavities and how best they may be used to enhance the completed model. Many pieces of driftwood contain very attractive colours, which are discovered only when the inequalities and blemishes of the exterior have been removed. Once when working on a piece of walnut root, I was thrilled to find black, orange and purple and an intermingling of colours impregnated into the basic colour of the wood. I discovered that any wood exposed to the action of sea water over a long period underwent two changes; one in colour and the other in texture. Changes in colour are due mainly to the dissolved mineral and chemical salts carried by the rivers into the oceans. Long immersion causes the wood to become infused with these salts. . . .

Cory soon realised that the North Coast of Cornwall was an excellent 'hunting ground', being wide open to the currents of the North Atlantic Ocean.

Where else except along that wild exposed sea board, for instance, would I have found that intricately shaped piece of Canadian maple which I carved into the final shape of a ballerina? Or the myrtle wood with its infused black and orange colours and which developed into a bird shape? Or again, the specimens of bog oak, the first of which I mistook for ebony, and which I stumbled across on the pebble ridges at Millook, with its gigantic and magnificent folded strata cliffs towering majestically into the sky?

Root wood I found to be especially adaptable. One shape, which I later discovered resembled Barbara Hepworth's 'Outer Space', resulted because, long ago, two lateral roots had been diverted from their natural courses, by a rock or other obstruction, and had linked together in a circular form. Then there was the curved and twisted piece of gorse root which had found its way into the ocean as a consequence of the erosion of our broken sandstone cliffs. The shape which evolved was so similar to Zadkin's commemorative monument, 'Jan Gat', which stands in the middle of Rotterdam, that one of my friends, on seeing the model, assumed (wrongly, of course) that it had been copied. This model has proved extremely valuable when demonstrating how curves and twists in abstract shapes can suggest experiences of life, e.g., cruelty, torture, suffering and death, which, incidentally, is what Zadkin set out to do!

Cory's is an especially vivid example of a peculiarly Cornish craft: one sees that the end product is literally alive with the feeling—the haunting presence—of the county of its creation. There are many other crafts that can equally be associated with Cornwall in a very physical way: for instance, a most obvious one, the serpentine momentoes produced at several small villages on the Lizard.

Rushwork is another interesting example, revived in Cornwall in the 1950's by the late Jeanne Stanley. It all began for her one afternoon when she sat on a stool in a farmyard making a waste-paper basket out of direct rushes from the borders of the River Fal.

A neighbour passing by stopped and said: 'Did 'ee know that be an old, old Cornish job?' And he went on to explain how the old folk used to 'traace' the rushes and make them into maunds for field work—'traacing' being plaiting or tressing the rushes, 'just like 'ee do traace a little maid's hair'. In the old days the rushworkers would take out pith and rub it in their hands to make the wicks for candles and fish-oil lamps. Farmers used rushes to thatch ricks, and housewives made mats for their blue stone floors.

At that moment rushcraft became alive for me. The only tools I wanted were sack needles, a ruler and sharp scissors. I could make baskets with no tools but my fingers as the American natives did. I had no textbook, but no book can teach as well as practical experience, and I have had plenty of that . . . The vagaries of Cornish Field rushes would fill a huge tome.

After that Miss Stanley searched into the history of Cornish rushwork, discovering that near Devoran, Falmouth, there was once a rush factory: that the Ancient Britons made rush baskets which were so admired by the Romans that they took them back to Italy (to this day Italians make rush trays in which to carry their fruit and vegetables); and that at one time Cornish children used to make their toys out of rushes, tiny baskets being favourites. Using all this knowledge Miss Stanley steadily developed her unusual art, and before her death was awarded the title of GWYADORES BRONNENNOW ('Weaver of Rushes') at the Cornish Gorsedd.

Weaving in general has enjoyed a notable revival in Cornwall, where the Cornwall Guild of Weavers alone has 60 members. Margery Hicks, secretary of the Guild, has given this interesting portrait of her craft's development:

One of the best traditional weavers in England lives at Mevagissey and opens her summer studio at Pentwean to visitors. Gladys Haymer has won many national weaving competitions; her work is meticulously perfect; she can show you samples of fine silk woven on a dobby-loom that have the elegance of eighteenth-century French Brocade. Studios like hers—and Miss Angove's, 'Jennifer', at Crantock—where the weaver can be seen working at the loom, are immensely attractive to those craft-hungry tourists who are weary of mass production, and rejoiced to find something worthier of Cornwall than a machine-made pisky to take home as a souvenir. Joe Marsland is an exuberant colourist who likes making cheerful but sophisticated dirndls that are made-up-to-order-on-the-spot by Betty, his wife, in their shop at Delabole. On the Wharf at St Ives, Mrs Pearson has an Aladdin's cave of crafts that keeps her too busy to weave except in the winter. Roseland has weavers at Portscatho and Veryan, besides the long established showroom of the Roseland Weavers, on the road to St. Mawes. At Perranuthnoe, Muriel Harvey has just woven a silk sash in the newly-evolved Cornish tartan, for the wife of the Grand Bard. At Mount Hawke, near Truro, Jack Inglis has a one-man industry; he makes knubbly shoulder-bags in brilliant colours and sturdy modern furnishing fabrics; his wife is his business manager; Heal's and Liberty's buy from them and they export dress material to America. With Joe Marsland they exhibited at the Royal Cornwall, and Dingles invited them to weave at a 'Crafts in the West' exhibition at Plymouth. Jack Inglis is in love with his craft; he works all day and every day, and says the day is not half long enough for his enjoyment.

Near Helston there is another one-man, ex-army officer industry. After twenty years' service with the Royal Engineers, John Madden was faced with the question of resettlement as a civilian. By chance he saw a loom, and was intrigued by the prospect of making his living as a craftsman . . . but could he make it pay? Would weaving educate three children? The story of how he resolved his doubts and overcame his difficulties and established the Tweenstream Weavers proves that anyone bold enough to enter into open competition with mass-production can successfully do so by speeding output with mechanical aids, but not allowing these to destroy the individual character of his work. At Praze, a retired engineer has harnessed the power of an old watermill to drive his loom; the inventor of the Raper Auto Leveller now devises ingenious attachments to be tried out on the looms at Tweenstream. On the North Coast we have another inventive craftsman—Guy Kraushaar, a retired bank manager from London. In his sail-loft workshop, with its splendid view of the coast from Port Isaac to Tintagel, is a loom that is a craftsman's dream of accurate adjustment: a Meccano construction plies threads by electricity, electric power winds bobbins.

In weaving, as in any other creative art, there must be experiment and, like all innovation, this is not universally acceptable. A wave of wall-hangings has swept over the country since America sent over a 'Weaving for Walls' exhibition. Weavers jettisoned conventional yarns overnight and abandoned formal processes; 'woven forms' became the thing, contrived by unusual means from unlikely material. Traditional weavers were disconcerted and inclined to cavil ... 'but this is not weaving ...' Fresh ideas should not be spurned, however; they open a new dimension and cause the mind—as Picasso says—to 'thrust forward into the unknown.' They enrich the craft. In Cornwall we have a gifted designer-craftsman in Win Evans of Bolingey, until lately lecturer in design at Redruth College of Art. One of her earliest wall-hangings, 'Nebula', after a two-year tour of Britain with our own 'Weaving for Walls' exhibition, has been bought by the Victoria and Albert Museum. It is a striking conception woven from aluminium strips on a groundwork of fiery scarlets, and has led to further American commissions for Mrs Evans and a place in the 'Young Britain' exhibition on Fifth Avenue. 'Colour Bar'—in wool, wood and Brazine rods—was a focus of interest and controversy at the Truro exhibition. Shown here, too, was her very first hanging, 'Tresco', in which the scimitar-shapes of eucalyptus leaves from the gardens of Tresco Abbey, in Scilly, are punctuated by dark blobs of bark picked up on St Agnes Beach, and held in a shimmering web of muted plum and gold and grey. This approach to weaving as an art form is shared by another of Cornwall's younger weavers, Lesley Hoskin. Married to a farmer and mother of a very young family, she literally rocks the cradle with one hand and weaves with the other. At Truro she showed a room-divider in split bamboo and willow and an imaginative tapestry called 'China Clay Hills.'

It was an embroiderer—a craft very close to weaving—who once gave one of the best explanations of the effect of Cornwall on a craftsman. Ermay Harvey James, in an article in the CORNISH REVIEW, wrote:

My childhood was spent in West Cornwall, near Hayle, and from that time the memory of shells and seaweed and fierce, frail wings seen against sand and sun-pierced water formed the unconscious bias towards a particular emphasis, a personal conception of reality, which emerged years later with the recognition of the remote connection between these images and the texture of thread on linen. It would be difficult to say exactly when and how this happened, but suddenly these things were connected and because of the connection one saw them like this instead of that. The past then was a source of richness, like buried treasure, which having lain in silence and darkness now became accessible.

Crafts are very much a normal and natural part of daily life in Cornwall: in many a small fishing-port or village, as well as in quite remote country areas—and in the market towns, too—the visitor is likely to find some craftsman at work down a side street, like the weavers at Crantock, at Pentwan, at Perranuthno, at Mount Hawke, and so on. Or, to take other crafts, there is a wrought-iron forge on the main road from Hayle into Lelant; on the Wharf at St Ives is the workshop from which emerges the fine, cleanly made peasant-type of furniture made by Robin Nance, son of the former Gorsedd Bard of Cornwall; while at boatyards in Falmouth and Penryn and Mevagissey old craftsmen produce beautiful Cornish luggers and other sailing-craft.

There are, in fact, endless examples that can be quoted of Cornish craftsmen at work. To conclude, however, one cannot do better than consider the phenomenal development of a particular craft which in many ways is perhaps the best known of all in Cornwall—pottery. There are, of course, historical reasons why this ancient craft is associated in particular with the county, for it was in the areas of mid-Cornwall and North Cornwall and North Devon that William Cookworthy first made his original discoveries of ball-clay which led to the development of such a major industry. And with clay being mined in the area it was perhaps only natural that small potteries should start up. In fact raw clay was to be found in various parts of the county a long time ago (and can still be dug up in such areas as St Hilary or St Erth, where the old clay-mines remain).

Today, the number of studio potteries at work in Cornwall is quite remarkable—at last count the figure was around 60, and increases every year. It is certainly most unlikely that any other English county has a half or probably even a quarter of that figure. In Stoke-on-Trent, of course, there are many more commercial potteries, but that is really a different industry, and the difference between it and the studio potteries such as those found in Cornwall has been well put by a leading exponent of the latter:

> The artist craftsman should be the natural source of contemporary applied design, whether he works in conjunction with industry or prefers, as most of us do, to carry out our ideas in clay, cotton, wood, glass, metal or leather, etc., mainly with our own hands and at our own tempo. The hand is the prime tool and it expresses human feelings intimately; the machine for quantity, cheapness and, at best, a marvellous efficiency, but it turns man into a modern slave unless it is counterbalanced by work which springs from the heart and gives form to the human imagination.

When Bernard Leach wrote those words he could well have been thinking of developments over the past 30 years of the Cornish studio potteries—and indeed the Leach Pottery at St Ives in particular. Founded in 1920, the Pottery still occupies the same premises, at the top of The Stennack, St Ives. Until 1937 the ware was fired in an old-fashioned wood kiln, but this has since been replaced by oil-burning kilns that produce a wide range of high-fired stoneware 'because it suits the conditions of modern life best and offers a wider field of suggestion and experiment.'

Not surprisingly the Leach Pottery and the distinguished reputation of its founder—and subsequently his sons, David and Michael Leach—drew many followers. From the beginning a deliberate policy of taking students was adopted, while in addition short courses are held periodically for art students. Altogether nearly 1000 students must have passed through the pottery, so that its influence has been considerable. The co-operative side of the venture has always been very important to Bernard Leach, who was himself trained in Japan, home of the cooperative pottery movement. He once said:

> At the Leach Pottery, by accepting the Cornish motto of 'one for all and all for one' and by making the workshop a *we* job instead of an *I* job, we appear to have solved our main economic problems as hand-workers in a machine age, and to have found out that it is still possible for a varied group of people to find and give real satisfaction because they believe in their work and in each other. To me the most surprising part of the experience is the realisation that—given a reasonable degree of unselfishness—divergence of aesthetic judgement has not wrecked this effort. When it comes to the appraisal of various attempts to put a handle on a jug, for example, right in line and volume and apt for purpose, unity of common assent is far less difficult to obtain than might have been expected.

Bernard Leach believes strongly that the educated craftsman of today is thrown up as a reaction against the over-mechanisation of labour at a certain stage following the Industrial Revolution, and that this kind of person possesses an insight into the epochs of man's culture and in his or her own workshop passes such influences through the mesh of personality. And he believes equally strongly that Cornwall, a unique place, offers a unique opportunity for craftsmanship to flourish. Today the Leach Pottery is by no means the largest concern of its kind in Cornwall—there are two studio potteries in Newlyn alone that perhaps employ more people—but it is true to say that the Leach influence has drawn many potters to Cornwall. This does not mean that copying has been slavish; for instance, stoneware is not all that common, and most of the Cornish potteries produce earthenware pots.

The visitor will not travel far without finding a studio potter at work. Here are just a few of them: The Tintagel Pottery in Sir Richard Grenville's old home at Bossinney; Michael Cardew's stoneware pottery at Wenlock Bridge, near Bodmin Moor; John Nash's pottery at Marazion, overlooking the wide sweep of Mount's Bay, and the nearby looming mass of St Michael's Mount; the Celtic Pottery and the Troika Pottery, both in former fish-cellars at Newlyn; Little Penderleath Pottery up on the moors at Nancledra, between Penzance and St Ives; the Polperro Pottery at the entrance to that famous and picturesque fishing port; the Millstream Pottery overlooking beautiful Fowey Harbour. . . . Several potters may also be found in the Craft Market, St Ives, one of several similar concerns which have recently developed in Cornwall, adding still further to a pleasant atmosphere of craftsmen at work.

Far from the hustle and bustle of the big cities, in a world where artists are taken for granted and accepted as a natural part of the landscape, the potters of Cornwall have learned to appreciate their good fortune. It is seldom that a potter ever leaves Cornwall: though, contrariwise, not a year goes by without another handful making the trek West, searching for that old barn, that former fish-cellar or some similar building suitable for converting into a pottery. This, indeed, is the trend among all crafts, for the Rural Industries Bureau confirms that more and more such people are moving into Cornwall. Not only is this one invasion that might surely be welcomed, for a change; it is a simple yet impressive proof of the scope of that mysterious net in which Cornwall seems to enmesh all kinds of creative workers.

VIII

The Timeless Land

POETS AND PAINTERS, novelists and actors, potters and weavers, musicians and composers, singers and bards . . . we have seen in the preceding chapters how various types of creative workers have been drawn to Cornwall, and its profound influence on their work and, indeed, on their lives. But in fact we have still only covered a part of the total area: there are many, many more categories and space precludes dealing with them all in detail. In concluding it may be relevant to touch on just one or two more significant examples.

Film-making is one that comes to mind almost automatically. Cornwall is nothing if not highly cinematic, and the film people have not been slow to comprehend this. Many people may still remember the wartime film, *Love Story*, starring Margaret Lockwood and James Mason, in which some of the major scenes were shot against the romantic background of the Minack Theatre. Not long afterwards an American company used Cornish location-shots in making Daphne du Maurier's *My Cousin Rachel*, with Olivia de Haviland in the star part (and a very young Richard Burton as her lover). There have in fact been a whole sequence of films which have been part or even wholly shot on location in various parts of Cornwall. Most recently and famous—or perhaps notorious—was Dustin Hoffman's *Straw Dogs*, for which the entire village of St Buryan was taken over as the permanent set for a weird story of lust, rape and murder. It is interesting in that the story was originally set in another part of Britain, but the director deliberately changed the venue to Cornwall as the most appropriate background for such a tale! And he was right, of course. If ever there was a background made for melodrama and Grand Guignol, then surely Cornwall must be the choice. One has only to stand on the cliffs at Land's End on a blustery afternoon—or struggle across the windblown sands below Hell's Mouth, at Godrevy—or scramble up the face of the dreaded Dodman Head in Roseland, with waves pounding the pitiless, jagged rocks below—to appreciate the powerful visual effect of such settings. Translated to the cinema screen they contribute startlingly to any film story, especially if it is one by such masters of suspense and menace or superstition as Daphne du Maurier, Hammond Innes, or Howard Spring.

There is a more interesting side to the link between film-making and Cornwall. We hear or read in the gossip-columns about the major film ventures. We do not always happen to catch the passing references to a wide variety of secondary feature-films which also chose Cornwall for their location. Some settings—notably, for instance, the Zennor cliffs near St Ives, or the Sennen Cove area by Land's End—are in almost constant demand for second feature films, short documentaries, or even advertising films. A friend of mine once earned £12 a day draping herself decoratively in a swimsuit on a boat moored in St Ives harbour, posing for a publicity film producing an advertising epic for a proprietary cornflake. When the film was finally shown she appeared for only two seconds, but the film-makers must have considered the considerable expense of taking a large unit down to Cornwall a justifiable outlay. And of course, so it was. There was about their film a freshness, an ordinariness, merely because of those genuine shots of waves curling over the sands of St Ives Harbour, those silhouettes of old fishing smacks—leaning on the harbour walls—above all, those magnificent sunsets over Clodgy Point. No artificial creations could have matched them, and indeed it would be difficult to imagine any more effective natural scenery in Britain.

Sometimes film companies have had the good sense to venture into less obvious locations. There have in fact been several documentary films shot around the background of the St Austell china-clay pits, those weird white mountains first seen on the horizon as you come across Bodmin Moor. Recently a British company making the film-treatment of the play *The Bed-sitting Room* by Spike Milligan and John Antrobus, used one of those vast cavernous clay-pits as the setting for this harshly satirical film. As a result of this enterprising choice a difficult transition of a confined theatrical conception to the wider medium was most effectively accomplished. Another instance of the same kind of thing was provided by the recent making of a science-fiction film by J. G. Ballard, based upon a story about the end of the world, set in the same futuristic-looking landscape of the clay pits.

Film actors and film actresses are notoriously superficial in their public comments, at least as presented by the press, but it is fair to say that they seem almost unanimous in their appreciation of the chance of filming in Cornwall. Many of them—like Patricia Neal the American character actress—have been back several times: some, like Pat Phoenix and Rita Tushingham, have actually bought houses in Cornwall. What they all comment on is exactly what the artists reiterate—the pleasantly unexpected lack of conventionality in Cornwall, the almost total lack of class-barriers, the persistent sense of a true community life. People are accepted, people go their own way: in an unusual world, the unusual ways of life are no longer so. The artists and actresses, with their flamboyant apparel and manners, really feel at home—as do the directors and their technicians. They express themselves more precisely about the relevance of the Cornish landscape, confessing that there is nowhere else in the British Isles, with the possible exception of some parts of Ireland, where there is the same combination of grandiose scenery and fine light, indeed an appropriate setting for drama and melodrama.

From film-making it is a small step to television. Here Cornwall has been much more frequently used—for after all, at Plymouth are the headquarters both of the South-west Region of the B.B.C., and of Westward Television. It is from here that cameramen travel out to obtain those dramatic shots of the keepers of the Wolf Lighthouse being relieved in gales; of a ship foundering off the Lizard; of searches for lost hikers on Bodmin Moor; or perhaps of some ancient bardic ceremony on top of Trencrom or Brown Willy. Photogenically, Cornwall is *always* newsworthy.

Then there are the documentaries: both companies make a feature of producing a regular supply of these—on the clay-pits, on the tin-mines, on the Lifeboat services, on Cornish crafts, on Ancient Cornwall, on villages sinking under the sand, and so on. Sometimes, too, London producers and units come down on a foray into regional territory—as recently when Stephen Peet made a film about a famous strike of the clay-workers in the St Austell area; or there is a local effort-extraordinary—as when Angela Rippon produced a fascinating Westward reconstruction of the barren life of a now 'dead' East Cornish mining village, *The Deserted Valley*.

Frequently units go out to sea with the Cornish fishing fleets from Newlyn or Looe . . . while there is sometimes the occasion of the arrival off Falmouth of some round-the-world-yachtsman, like Francis Chichester or Robin Knox-Johnson, who inevitably, made their first landsight off Cornwall.

This, of course, is one of Cornwall's secret weapons, or if you like, trump-cards. The meaning of the familiar phrase bandied about so much in West Cornwall, 'First and last' becomes fully comprehensible. If you are drinking in the *last* pub in England (at Sennen) then you are also drinking at the *first* pub in England. Either way, there is an element of the unusual, the extraordinary, about such an event. After all it is not every day that you *do* drink in either the first or last pub in a country. Similarly there are not many parts of Britain where you *can* see the world's crack express train finish up against buffers that literally mark the end of the line, as is the case in the Victorian-style station at Penzance. Again, to speak of 'Land's End' along the central South Coast of England, with the neighbouring coastline of France only about 60–70 miles away, would seem ludicrous—as it would on the North Coast, with Holland and Northern Europe just over the horizon. But Land's End, *Cornwall*, with some 3000 miles between your solitary figure on the beach and the nearest mainland, really is the Land's End.

Some of these unusual characteristics have been captured marvellously in television's twin but older art form, radio. Here, where the visual angle has to be forgotten, skilful producers and directors have managed to capture the sounds of Cornwall on tape and microphone. I once made use of this medium myself when I wrote *Cornwall for the Cornish*, a feature programme broadcast by the B.B.C., appropriately enough, on April Fool's Day. By using sound effects of all kinds of normal Cornish life—the Helston Flora Dance, a Cornish rugby match, beach events, carnivals, etc.,—and linking with a satirical commentary, I was able to portray a comic version of UDI in Cornwall, the county being taken over by the Nationalists and run as an independent country. I need only add the obvious comment that such a programme could hardly have been made of any other part of England—and we see once again; how *different* is Cornwall.

With microphone and tape-recorder, B.B.C. reporters have been down the Cornish mines, out in lifeboats, mingled with holiday-makers, attended regattas and carnivals and festivals, and generally created a word-picture of Cornwall that has been fit, in its way, to put beside the films and the television documentaries. Few who listen or watch any of these are likely to remain unmoved. Whether cinematically or orally, the impact of Cornwall is an intriguing one. In my experience it is rather as when one sees those travel-films of the Greek Isles, or the Yugoslavian coast: the moment people see Cornwall 'writ bold'—and especially in colour—they cannot wait to go and see it for themselves. And after all, is this so very surprising? Let us consider just two of the many facets of the county. What about, for instance, its first dramatic area encountered soon after driving up out of Launceston—Bodmin Moor. As Michael Tresillian once said:

A shoulder of land rises hiding Rough Tor—and I am reminded that Bodmin

Moor tends to be obscured in another context. Thousands of words are written eulogising Cornwall. The majority of those words, though, are written by men drawn by the roar of the Atlantic. They laud our long, indented coastline. They write about beaches, coves, harbours, cliffs, estuaries and the surge of the sea. They forget the weird, wild world of the moor. Bodmin Moor admittedly cannot match Dartmoor in sheer height. But is landscape quality to be assessed in mere feet? Does the tape-measure take into account atmosphere? Or age? Or history?

Once the Moor—or to be precise St Breward, formerly Simonsward—was the most thickly populated area in Cornwall. Three thousand years before the stable birth at Bethlehem, ancient man encamped here. A thousand years later the Bronze Age people, a more sophisticated race, arrived; King Arthur's so-called Hall, a rectangular enclosure, is thought to belong to this era. Then came the Celts, from whom we Cornish are descended. The Celts with their knowledge of the wheel which they employed for ploughing, were the pioneer farmers. Fields and place-names are reminders of their contribution. Tin was mined on the Moor. Rakes remain—huge furrows in the ground made by miners—but the noise of labour died long ago. De Lank Quarry, though, flourishes.

Cathedral of the Moor is the church of St Nonna's at Altarnum—the biggest parish in the county: 15,000 acres. The village itself is a little more than a street of aged cottages, surrounded by elms and beeches, but eyes automatically go to St Nonna's 130-ft tower. The tallest of all Cornish churches, it took more than a generation to construct. The stone that built this church came from three sources; from unquarried stone lying on the moor, from the previous Norman Church and from the Mansion of the Trelawney family, who in the fifteenth century moved to Trewlawne. St Nonna's gems are 79 beautifully carved bench-ends. They date from 1510 to 1530 and are carved with the Instruments of the Passion, a man with a cauldron, another with bagpipes, a fiddler, a mixture of parish worthies, common sights and renaissance designs and religious themes.

Another writer, C. E. Vulliamy, in *Unknown Cornwall*, threw light on another romantic corner of the Moor,

Nowhere on earth are there landscapes more austerely beautiful, more wonderful in their change of mood and colour, or more splendid in outline. The pool in its placid moods when it becomes a mirror reflecting the forms of moor and cloud, has a charm so powerful, yet so elusive, that it can only be conveyed to you in pictures: the limits of descriptive writing are soon reached when we are dealing with the sublimely simple in landscape, and the charm of Dozmary is composed visually of the simplest elements—water, sky and earth. Indeed the value of much of the Cornish landscape is essentially a pictorial value, a value of breadth and space, of sky and cloud, of wide surfaces and large, simple forms. The landscapes of literature are otherwise; crowded with detail or incident or movement.

Dozmary, of course, is that saucer-like depression to the South-west of Fowey Valley, a mile in circumference and 500 yds across, which was supposed to be the bottomless pool into which Sir Belvedere, in reluctant obedience to the dying King Arthur, traditionally threw the sword of Excalibur. It is also associated with another legend, that of the evil John Tregeagle, who was charged by the spirits for his misdeeds and sentenced endlessly to bail out Dozmary with a leaky limpet-shell. He was so tormented by the impossibility of his task that he fled to Roche Rock, hammering and howling to be let in. Children of later generations used to be told that storm noises were Tregeagle and his hell-hounds hunting on the Moor . . . No wonder the mere name Bodmin Moor immediately conjures up a sense of a brooding, haunted world—a setting uniquely Cornwall.

At the other extreme, where better to look than at the opposite end of the county, at Land's End itself? People who have lived a long time in Cornwall come to realise that many other spots all around the Cornish coast—places like the North Cliffs between Padstow and Newquay, or Portquin or Port Isaac, or the Manacle Rocks off Helford, or Kynance Cove on the Lizard—have settings just as picturesque, just as majestic, as Land's End. The fact is nothing could be more overdone, more 'touristy' than Land's End, with its huge car-parks, hotels, gifts shops, and so on. Nevertheless, despite all these trappings, you have only to walk a little way along those cliffs, to lose yourself from the coaches and package-tours among the soft moss and heather of the winding paths to Nanjizel, and it will be surprising if you do no begin to feel ancient stirrings in your imaginative bones. No wonder Ruth Manning-Sanders wrote about her feeling that drowned sailors could still be heard hailing their names above the moaning of the waters. At Land's End, in the world of the Enys Dodman Rock, The Bishop, and the distant Longships Lighthouse, the waters do moan, and it is not difficult to believe that many drowned sailors must have called their names in pitiful supplication (weirdly, to this day, the Runnelstone Light Buoy emits a strange moaning sound as the wind whistles through its structure).

It is at Land's End, looking out on a red sunset evening towards the distant romantic humps of the Scilly Isles (of which there are 200) that one remembers, hauntingly, the legend of the lost land of Lyonesse . . . for there it is, lying between you and the Scillies. In *Curious Cornwall* a local author, B. Trevail, paints this picture of the spectator's feelings as he watches the tide rising around most of those little islets of the Scillies:

> It is an unusual experience, even to the island Britisher, to watch this vast fleet of rocks vanish one by one beneath a rising tide; at low water they are to be numbered in hundreds, whilst at high relatively few remain and there is perhaps for the more imaginative a brief feeling of panic as the inexorable rise of

water continues. The sea between these many closely grouped islets, a clear and marvellous blue in summer but in winter a seething mass of treachery, is thus so shallow that only the slightest elevation of the sea bed would make of them one many-pinnacled granite island. In the same way, the waters between Scilly and Land's End are none too deep, and the slightest uplift of the ocean floor here would also produce dry land—and so there would re-emerge once more the magical and long lost land of Lyonesse.

For legend has it that such a land once existed: a land of great fertility, inhabited by a beautiful race of people who built many splendid cities—does not the dreaded Seven Stones reef mark the site of one of them?—and some 140 equally marvellous churches whose bells from time to time may be heard beneath the sea, gently tolling with the rocking waves. One single night, some 900 years ago, the whole of Lyonesse was overcome by a vast inundation from the sea, which flooded over all but its highest peaks, catching the sleeping people unawares and engulfing the cities and churches in rapid succession. It is said that only two living creatures survived this disaster—a man named Trevelyan, of Basil, near Launceston, who was able to flee before the rising wall of water on his swift white horse and reached dry land safely at Perranuthnoe.

And so Lyonesse disappeared beneath the sea, engulfed by a wide stretch of glittering sea that separated the newly created cliffs of the Land's End and the just-born Scilly Isles barely visible on the far horizon. Mount's Bay fishermen at one time—perhaps still—would tell you that on clear nights near the Seven Stones the roofs of houses were visible beneath the water, while there is other more down-to-earth collaboration, both historical and geological, of the drowning of Lyonesse. The Saxon Chronicle even states that 'the Lionesse was destroyed on November 11, 1099'—but then who wants proof; we must all be permitted to dream.

In Cornwall—on Bodmin Moor, at Land's End, among the bejewelled Scilly Isles—we are not only permitted but encouraged to dream. Cornwall is a dreamer's world, complete, on occasions, with the authentic nightmare. In this granite land we are continually made to feel aware not merely of an immediate past, but of a huge and endless remote past stretching in the infinite. Thus still to this day, all over Cornwall, there stand some 400 of the old Celtic crosses, a later derivative of the Bronze Age menhirs, or standing-stones. These crosses had various purposes—to mark holy places, in memory of the dead, as boundary-stones or guide-posts. Carved out of very old, grey granite, crude and simple, often surprisingly large (with shafts up to 20 ft), these crosses speak across centuries. Put your hands on their rough surfaces—or for that matter put your hands on the great granite surface of some of the stones on top of Trencrom, or Castle Dinas, or Chysauster—and you will be a dullard if you do not imagine a tremble of ancient communication. There are indeed, as Shakespeare said, 'sermons in stones.' As Sir George P. Christopher suggested, expounding on the poet's phrase:

He was looking not at the hard seemingly immobile and unanswering exterior of the stones, but at something about them which was beyond even the magic of his own muse to express except in the terse phrase into which he put the whole volume of inner hidden things which man, consciously or unconsciously, envisages when he looks at these emblems of 'the rock whence ye were hewn'. What Cornishman, returning to his Motherland, can gaze unmoved upon the ancient, untidy, formless and apparently purposeless masses of boulders as he proceeds on his homing journey after crossing the Tamar?

If Shakespeare could not find the magic words, then I am hardly likely to do so: this book, alas, ends as it began, without satisfactorily defining the meaning of 'the timeless land'. But then perhaps to do so would be a contradiction in terms. There would be no mystery if one already knew by heart those 'sermons in stones'—both the sermons and the stones would become ordinary mundane things. It is the same with my title. As well as I have been able to, it captures something truthful about Cornwall, in its own exasperatingly loose terms. In one sense the words mean nothing—in another they mean everything. And that, I have striven to suggest, is what Cornwall is all about. Officially it is no more than another authorised county with its own county council, a county hall, a High Sheriff and a variety of perfectly ordinary commonplace institutions. Unofficially, it is an unknown land, a separate country, a world apart. The mystery is the paradox; or if you prefer, the paradox is the mystery. At least, as I hope I have managed to demonstrate, it is impossible to take a place like Cornwall for granted; somehow, even in its mere comtemplation, one is reminded of the current catchphrase: *And now for something quite different . . .*

The creative artist, a being of instinct and intuition, has always recognised that factor. What was it D. H. Lawrence wrote? 'We go to Cornwall in the morning . . .' Instinctively he saw it as beginning a new life altogether. And this is precisely what living in Cornwall has meant for dozens, indeed hundreds, of creative artists of many kinds. Those who have come and stayed have often been puzzled at the almost mysterious way in which they have been drawn; equally they have come to recognise that, in turn, they have derived some strange kind of sustenance from the land of their choice. The fact that this is so is really beyond dispute; and to demonstrate it I have quoted a formidable number of testimonies.

When I have referred to Cornwall as 'the creative country' then, I have meant my words literally. This is perhaps the message of this book, if message one must have: namely that the creative forces in Cornwall are two-way. Creative workers have been drawn and they have brought with them great talents: but in return, they have been given something, too. This was expressed very succinctly by Sven Berlin, the sculptor, when he described the excitement he felt when the Cornish sea 'got into' a shape he was carving, how 'it goes charging through the whole of the stone and a man, as if by magic is transformed into an ocean with rocks and tides, shells and caves, a sea dragon.' It was Cornwall, Sven Berlin declared, that helped to realise and develop his entire ability to create living things in stone.

I do not personally think it would be going too far to say that it would seem unimaginable that any genuine creative artist could visit Cornwall and fail to be profoundly influenced. Fortunately we are often able to witness visually such influences—in a Ben Nicholson drawing, in a Barbara Hepworth sculpture, in a Sydney Graham poem, in a Du Maurier novel, in a Leach pot or one of Cory's transformed pieces of driftwood. We see it most dramatically in the oil paintings of a modernist like Margo Maeckleberghe who, asked to state how and why Cornwall attracted painters, put it like this:

> The crystal clear light . . . gives everything a new meaning, form and structure of the landscape is defined and enlarged by it. And atmosphere . . . very stimulating, strange, strong, primitive, beautiful . . . all these and much more besides. Words are really inadequate. The most important part to me is this mysterious X, an artist must *feel* about a place to paint it and be true to his art. Light, atmosphere, shimmering of pale, bleached grasses, surging half seen rocks, mist, rain, storm and sun on moors and headlands and, of course, skies, skies and skies . . .

There is no more to be said. In the end is the beginning, as it were. The timeless land has been, is and will be until forever—barring another accident like Lyonesse. And as long as it is here, so in its strange, magnetic way, it will continue to draw into its granite world artists of all kinds, from all parts. They will come, they will marvel—and if we are lucky, they will produce new wonders, new masterpieces.

And after all, of how many other English counties could we make so large and confident a prediction?